No, I don't work in the kitchen

No, I don't work in the kitchen

Surviving war-torn Afghanistan for three years

Veersen Bhoolai

Published by Tablo

Published in 2021 by Tablo Publishing.

FIRST EDITION

Publisher and wholesale enquiries: orders@tablo.io

20 21 22 23 LSC 10 9 8 7 6 5 4 3 2 1

Table of Contents

*Thank you to Joe, Shameed and Suren who encouraged me
to believe that this could be a book.*

Chapter 1

Off to Afghanistan BABY!!

If anyone had ever told me that I would one day live in war-torn Afghanistan, I would have laughed my head off.

However, if they had said that I would also live in Istanbul for close to a decade, I would have laughed at that too.

Well here I was, after eight years in Istanbul on my way to Kunduz via Kabul to work as a journalist for the United Nations.

Roughly one year before in September of 2008 my friend Aysel had suggested I apply for the job. We had just finished having a coffee at the Gloria Jeans Café at the end of Istiklal Avenue. As she walked out, she looked back at me, "You know we have a vacancy. Why don't you apply?"

I looked at her in surprise.

"Are you sure? I have just been part timing for the last decade."

"Yeah. Of course. I do the job and I am telling you you're qualified."

She sent me a link and I filled out the exhaustive forms and detailed history that they required. I was told that I would have to be vetted by the UN in terms of security clearance and this could take about six months or more.

I found myself only half wishing that I would get the job. If I did, I would be paid a minimum of ten thousand US dollars tax free plus perks. If not, I would move on to Vietnam to teach, make a lot less money but probably be so happy.

Finally, on August 5, I received my Security Clearance from the NATO Office in Belgium. I would be working specifically the International Security Assistance Force (ISAF) although a UN force there to protect projects by the UN, they were basically being controlled by NATO.

Now it was off to Afghanistan BABY!!!

First Day - Sept. 17

I got to the airport and everything went reasonably smoothly despite my overweight baggage.

Surprisingly, I got stopped by Turkish customs because there was some irregularity with the stamping of my passport the last time I left and entered Turkey.

I finally just showed them my NATO work Docs. and assured them I was leaving Turkey for good.

I had been waiting for a year to leave Turkey, yet when I took off on the plane and saw the lights of Istanbul, I actually felt kind of sad. I had spent most of the decade there. In some ways I had become more familiar with Istanbul than my hometown of Toronto. No more nargile water pipe or Turkish cuisine such as Tantuni or Kokoreç.

Two nice Turkish guys sat next to me on the plane. They were shocked to hear me speak Turkish to the stewardess. Upon learning that I was from the Caribbean, they made sure to tell me how much they liked the film Pirates of the Caribbean. I assisted them in immigration as they couldn't understand the officer when he spoke English to them. Basically, they were truck drivers who had been hired to drive a big rig from Germany to Turkey.

They then asked me to carry some extra cigarettes through customs for them :-)

Once we got through, they offered me a carton of cigarettes as a thank you. However, I politely declined as I don't smoke.

Now I was in Cologne at midnight. My flight was supposed to leave at 6:30 on September 18. The rest of my trip would be on a military plane. This is the protocol even though there are quicker ways to travel.

I thought I would go to the military airport and chill. As I came out of the civilian airport everybody around me was speaking Turkish. I went to the taxi drivers and asked if they spoke English, they kind of nodded and started speaking Turkish to each other :-)

I had been given a link for the military airport that didn't work. Well I learnt something that night, Zulu time should not be mistaken for standard time. I got to this empty ass airport at almost one in the morning. I was told to come back that my flight would leave at 10:30 am local time.

As the airport link didn't work, I simply had to go back to the civilian airport kill six hours and hope that I wasn't being jerked around.

I killed the six hours and came back at 7:30 am. Some German soldiers immediately helped me with my bags - nice fellows. They told me the plane would leave at 12:30 and that I could go to the restaurant upstairs.

I got on a huge commercial looking flight, staffed with only military personnel. About 180 German soldiers and seven odd civilians.

Six hours later we arrived in Termez, Uzbekistan. This was a military camp specifically for the Germans as part of the ISAF effort against the Taliban. Got some dinner, chatted with some civilians and went to sleep in a tent with seven other fellows. No pillows, so I rolled up my jacket and used it as one. Not the best option but it got the job done. However the tent did have electricity and air conditioning. They were also nice enough to give us big, thick, brown blankets.

Sept. 19 – We got up around 5:30 am for breakfast. Whilst in the canteen, I saw a German soldier, a handsome black fellow with the name Lara on his jacket. I told him that in my country it's a very famous name and why. He asked me where I was from and then mentioned that his parents are from Venezuela. So I told him to rest assured that he possessed quite a celebrated surname. Basically Brian Lara was the Michael Jordan of cricket and that even President Obama wanted to meet him. He and his German friends smiled. I made sure to tell him to google the name before walking off.

We were supposed to depart at 7 am but actually left at 8 am as the plane didn't arrive on time. Imagine my surprise - a military aircraft. It looked some big ass green cargo plane. I was actually a little nervous.

The bags were strapped to the floor and we sat facing each other on the side of the plane. I made some friends with some Dutch technicians and a Filipino-American, Mark who worked with them.

They were old hat at this. Mark gave me ear plugs for the ride and advised me to keep them as I would need them again. The take off and flight had me nervous as hell but the calmness of those around me helped me to keep calm myself. Twenty minutes later we were in Mazar-e-Sharif in Northern Afghanistan. We were almost there.

Chapter 2

Arrival in Kabul and Aysel's Turkish Syndrome

Sept. 19 - In Mazar-e- Sharif. Arrived about 8:20 am.

I had been travelling for about two days with very little sleep. However the five hours I had gotten the night before kept me going.

After 24 hours of travelling, the one and a half hour wait at MeS was no biggie. There was a reasonably nice cafe/departure lounge - considering I was at an army base. You could get coffee and sandwiches and watch their satellite TV.

I had a great chat with the Dutch guys and then we were off again. It was surreal to watch some of the soldiers either in fatigues or casually dressed with weapons/rifles strapped to their bodies. All of the soldiers and some civilians were wearing a bullet proof vest and helmet.

The one-hour ride on the military aircraft was a pain. Boring!! Some around me slept or read a book. A lot of the soldiers simply went to sleep with their rifles tucked between their legs.

After one excruciating hour I had arrived. I used the local phone to contact my friend Aysel who incidentally is my boss. She had advised me to contact her directly as she would ensure my pickup would be quicker. Because of security precautions and my newness to the area, they wanted to come for me in some sort of armoured vehicle.

The usual wait is about one to two hours while they scour for a ride. Aysel told me it should take them about an hour. I waited at the coffee shop with the Dutch guys, who were on their way to Kandahar in the south, a very dangerous place. They were enjoying an eight-hour transit wait.

They gave me some advice on adapting to my new environs.

One tip they had mentioned whilst still on the plane was "If you are going to be working for ISAF, you should meet Rebecca. She is really nice," said one of the Dutchmen.

They explained that like me she was from Canada. "Yeah, but call her Becky," said Mark. "That is what she prefers. She is really nice and a very beautiful woman."

I had no idea who this woman was but with the more than ten thousand odd personnel deployed to Afghanistan, I made a note to myself to look out for "Becky."

Aysel finally showed up 90 minutes after our call.

I had been looking forward to seeing her again. We had first me roughly 18 months before in Istanbul. There was a website where locals and foreigners could exchange idea on a variety of topics. She and I had communicated in terms of a Turkish-English language exchange. It was the first time I had ever done this with a stranger on the internet. I had no idea how that decision would have an astounding effect on my life.

She had been a TV reporter in Ankara and was now an ISAF journalist in Afghanistan. I was fascinated by her accomplishments as I myself was in the same occupation. We had a great chat on MSN. We met on Istiklal Avenue which was the centre of much action in Istanbul and coincidentally where I worked.

She was a pleasant attractive woman with tanned, olive skin, long, light brown hair halfway down her back and a warm smile.

We had a great chat over some beers and then went to another bar and polished off two bottles of red wine. She told me about her accomplishments. Her family was a reputable one, her father was a former Minister in the Turkish government, her Uncle was the Civilian Head of NATO in Afghanistan and her sister was a successful Doctor working abroad.

This was a woman who not only had IQ but EQ as well. Her English was not really good enough for the job but during the job interview if the conference call got too tough, she would pretend to have technical difficulties, "What! What! Can you speak up please? I can't hear you."

She would scratch the phone and then disconnect. They would call back and in a one-hour interview she had technical difficulties three times.

Once she had arrived in Afghanistan, she was sent to the Kunduz Provincial Reconstruction Team (PRT). As a civilian woman she was given special attention, she had her own office and sleeping quarters which no man would have been privy to. Too paranoid to speak a lot to the officers around her, she would bury her head in a book to make it look as if she were busy. She even had a friend proofread her English before sending it to Head Quarters.

As she was able to take leave regularly, I would see her often during the next year. As time progressed, it was obvious that she had taken a liking to me. Although the attraction wasn't mutual, I couldn't understand why. This was an attractive, intelligent, nice woman and a fellow journalist to boot. We would spend hours in each other's company and not be bored. I was happy to have a serious relationship with the right woman and being in my early forties I was aware that I wasn't going to look youthful and handsome forever.

I never encouraged anything but one night in December of 2008, she and two friends met me at a bar. I had seen her a few hours earlier and now she had done up her hair and even had Botoxinjected into her lips all in one afternoon.

I looked at her in amazement that anyone could affect such change in just a few hours.

"I am a woman," she replied with a smile.

Dressed in a simple blouse and a mini skirt, she sat next to me, she got drunk in an hour and held my hand under the table, putting it on her leg and held it there.

Her friends were unaware. I didn't know quite what to do. However, she was drunk and no one could see so I just let it happen.

By March of 2009 things had changed. Aysel had started a romance with a colleague. He was the Forward Media Team Leader in Kandahar province. Our department was the FMT and we had a leader in most provinces working with a local staff.

He had been besotted with her for quite a few months. He had even joked one day that the only reason he would renew his contract was only "if Aysel marries me."

As she put it, "I turned my head and looked at this short, ugly man making this joke about me."

However, with both in Kabul, they had dinner one night. She was impressed with his intellect. Drunk, they went back to her hotel room. She looked at him and made it very clear, "This is only physical."

However, "He is so intelligent. I really like him. So we are a couple now."

When she visited me in May, I was glad to hear that. It meant less pressure on me when we went out. We had exchanged emails during the months leading up to September both anxious to finally meet in Kabul and continue our friendship there.

We had agreed in late 2008 that I would edit her reports as she still had a lack of confidence in her English. I must have done a good job because a few months later, she was offered the position Head of the Forward Media Team. They were impressed not just with the quality of her work but her "improved English." She made it clear that she did not think her English was where it should be and that she would accept the Deputy position. Consequently, Karl Schmeling, a German, applied and received the senior position. Therefore, when I arrived, she would be greeting me as my boss.

Now. Finally!! Here we were.

Aysel showed up with Karl and we had a coffee and a chat and then were off.

The first thing they did before entering the vehicle was to give me my bullet proof vest and helmet. That vest weighs a great deal. If you ever see someone actually running with a bullet proof vest on, be impressed. I had never actually put one on before so Karl was nice enough to do it for me. I felt like a bit of a retard, like some silly child, while he did it. But once learnt, I would never need help again.

We dropped my bags off at Aysel's hotel, the Heetal Plaza and then were off to ISAF Headquarters. They wanted to get my paperwork done quickly as the date for posting that month's earning was at an end. That way I could actually receive my salary for September.

I was taken to the CPO (Civilian Personnel Office) and introduced to everyone. Amazingly, Becky worked in this office. When I explained that she had been mentioned to me before I had even entered Afghan airspace, she blushed and hid her face behind her computer as her colleagues all had a good laugh.

She truly is an attractive woman, slim, naturally tanned skin, medium length, slightly curly black hair, she reminded me of some of the women of the Caribbean.

She and Jess (an Ethiopian) are both from Canada, Montreal and Ottawa, respectively. They will be my major point of contact regarding most HR matters.

ISAF had many reconstruction projects going on throughout the country, such as roads, schools, hospitals and a number of social and education programs. I would be working in the PSYOPS (Psychological Operations) Department. Specifically it was known as CJPOTF, Combined Joint Operations Task Force. PSYOPS is basically using information to influence the public, organisations and the government. In layman's terms it could be called Public Relations or PR with a dash of exaggeration here and there. Some might even say with a dash of propaganda. I wasn't aware of the exaggeration part yet and I would never need to in my three years in Afghanistan.

CJPOTF had a Media arm, Radio, TV and Print. I would be working for the Print section. The newspaper was called Sada-e-Azadi, all stories were published in Dari, Pashto and English in the same issue.

There wasn't much for me to do as I had not yet been sent to Kunduz. I spent the next few days getting debriefings. I was tired as hell listening to loads of technical talk and just nodding my head and signing documents. However, Aysel was there with me every step of the way.

As I didn't really know many people there, I tagged along with her quite a bit. She knew the HQ well and instead of taking the paths would just cut through behind or between the buildings. It was confusing at first but got easier as the days went by. Although I had never noticed her in Istanbul, now seeing her as a woman in authority, she seemed a lot more attractive.

In my fatigue I had to hear that my posting, Kunduz, has become a little dangerous and is under rocket attack every week. "But don't worry it's not dangerous. The rockets just make a lot of noise. It's like BOOM, BOOM, hello, welcome to Kunduz," explained Jess.

BOOM,   BOOM,   hello,   welcome   to
Kunduz?????????.........................WTF!!!????

Aysel later explained that no one really gets hurt. The Taliban only have a few rockets. There might be max, three attacks a week and really, only about five or six rockets for the whole week. Only one person has been killed *in the camp* in the last year or so. Outside the camp however, that's a different story.

Staying at the same hotel as Aysel, we enjoyed our chats during the first two days. We had spent months in Istanbul talking about when we finally got together in Afghanistan how we would enjoy the different drinking spots. On the first night, she took me to a Lebanese restaurant. It was just a few hundred metres from our hotel but Aysel NEVER went anywhere without her driver. As she put it, you never knew when there could be an attack. It would take me just three months to realize how wise she was.

The owner immediately brought us free slices of meat, bread and salad. Apparently, he had a bit of a crush on her and she always got good service. If you happened to be with her, then you too got some freebies.

The restaurant was located in a very affluent neighbourhood of Afghanistan, as some put it, "the Afghan version of Bel Air." It certainly was a posh area, housing some of the country's high- ranking Ministers and diplomats. A North American might not be easily impressed at first glance, seeing all the potholes and a few of the homes in disrepair. But one has to understand that this is a city that has been ravaged by war. As Aysel put it, some people don't bother to repair some of the damage as it may only happen again.

I was introduced to the owner, Kamal Hamade, he was a charming and generous host. Aysel explained my nerves as a newcomer to Kabul. He laughed.

"Oh, this is nothing. I had a restaurant in Tripoli, Libya. You could hear the rockets passing overhead every day." The way he dismissively laughed he might as well have been talking about passing cows.

Apparently, this was how he made his money. He would go to war torn areas, knowing that the soldiers and expats were in need of certain services and luxuries. He seemed to be doing quite well.

In addition, he was not sparse with security. There were a huge number of sandbags piled up in front of the restaurant, reminding me of a World War I movie. There were four armed men at the entrance. You knocked on a steel door and entered a tunnel that also seemed to be made of steel, walked about 20 feet and knocked on another steel door and an armed guard let you in. He had at least eight security guards that I could see. I was impressed and thought to myself this man is well protected. I was a novice regarding Kabul and would later find out that such measures couldn't really stop the Taliban if they were determined.

Everything was going well with Aysel, I was so appreciative of her extra attention and it really helped me to settle in. Then on the third day it happened, she became Turkish.

We had had dinner at the hotel's restaurant, the menu wasn't the greatest but the Spaghetti Bolognese was acceptable. After dinner we sat in the garden which was between the restaurant and our rooms, we would drink and chat there. She was showing me some info regarding the location of different camps in Afghanistan. We were sitting side by side and our legs were touching. Suddenly, she got up and sat opposite me and just smiled. Any other foreigner may not have understood what had just happened but I had lived in Turkey for eight odd years and I was quite familiar with different aspects of their culture.

As someone who had lived in five countries prior to Afghanistan, I was aware that you did not judge others by your cultural norms. However, every once in a while, I had to shake my head. Many Turkish women despite appearing to be Western, being well educated and amiable can become idiots once they get a boyfriend. Women who joked and socialised with you, would now look the other way when they saw you and if you asked them a question, give you a sarcastic, weary answer and turn away.

Aysel's Turkish syndrome had now commenced. She then took on a more formal approach that night. Her boyfriend, Mustaffa, was scheduled to fly in from his camp in a few days. For the rest of the week she behaved quite formally. If I said good morning, she would answer in a passive manner and then turn away. She only spoke to me if necessary. The friendly, outgoing nature was gone. I was not completely surprised but I sure was disappointed. Not all Turkish women become stoic when they have a boyfriend or husband and I had thought Aysel above such childish behaviour.

For the next few nights, I dodged having dinner with her as I usually had an afternoon nap. Our rooms were side by side but she didn't speak to me now unless it was regarding work.

Mustafa showed up on September 23. Aysel knocked on my door and invited me to come and meet him. Trinidad & Tobago was playing hosts Egypt in the World Youth Cup of football so I made it clear she had to wait.

I came out and greeted him after the match. I was unimpressed. He was quite opinionated. He was critical of some of his colleagues as he did not deem them real journalists. He on the other hand had worked for the CBC Radio in Montreal.

He then turned to me, "Do you have any Journalism qualifications?"

"I hope so. I went to school, graduated and they gave me a Diploma. I have also been practicing my profession for the last 19 years."

He then went on to give me some examples of the incompetence he had to put up with. In addition, the Editors at HQ had given him the nickname "Drama Queen."

Being tucked away in our respective bases, I would only see my colleagues from time to time. It would take me more than a year to realize that Mustafa was actually quite an intelligent fellow and also very nice, despite his odd dramatic moments. ☺

Chapter 3

Acclimatizing and Don't Touch the Women

Sunday September 27, 2009

Well the first week is done. I met the Commander of my division earlier this week, a tall German fellow, Colonel Klose, seven feet tall and exceedingly polite, everybody likes him. He wanted to have a one on one with me.

I guess because he is a high-ranking Colonel and basically my boss, I was a bit nervous. He said, "Let's go outside. I don't like this office," and all I could think is

please get this over with. However, he is a very nice man. He asked me about my professional background. He explained that I might have some problems in the Kunduz (KDZ) Camp and if I was unable to solve them, to let him know. He made it clear that regarding the Commander at KDZ, "I have a superior rank so he will listen to me."

I had originally been posted to Kandahar, arguably the most dangerous place on the planet. However, this is the one time Aysel used her influence to help me.

She did not want the others to know we had been friends prior to my taking the job as they may have misconstrued how I actually got it. When she heard about sending me to Kandahar, she somehow influenced Karl to send me to Kunduz instead.

As she later told me, "I am the one who told Veersen to come here to Afghanistan. If he dies out there in Kandahar, I will feel guilty."

At the time I appreciated the gesture. However, what I would later find out was that it was the worst thing she could have done. The Kandahar Camp is like an independent city with over twenty thousand people living there. It is well equipped with restaurants, cinemas and has its own functioning airport that make regular international flights. On the other hands, many of the other camps were not really built for comfort and in the long run, it can have an effect on you psychologically.

The soldiers here in general are quite cordial always saying hello. The exception may be the ones from Eastern Europe. I don't know if it's my skin colour or just their way but I don't dwell on it too much.

Ironically, the lone bit of attitude or rudeness I have experienced is from the Canadians. Each country at the base has a National Support Element (NSE). They have some special services for their citizens on the base, e.g., cafe, store, postal service etc.

I asked to use to go to the internet room. The response I got from the officer was "Why?"

"Because I want to use the net."

"Why?"

"Because I am a Canadian citizen."

"Oh, it's not working right now, only the email."

I realize to some in this part of the world, I don't look like the average Canadian. In Canada I would shake my head at the ignorance. However, here maybe I should cut him some slack due to the appearance of the locals etc.

I mentioned it to Becky and Jess at the Civilian Personnel Office. They just shook their head. The Somalian is as black as pitch so he's well aware of

the ignorance. But as he put it, our colour allows us to blend outside :-)

Coincidentally, I called a taxi yesterday. When it finally arrived and I started walking towards it, the driver shook his head as if to say not for you. When he called to confirm that my taxi was there and I answered the phone just metres from his car, you could see the shock on his face. You have to be careful with which taxis you take. Not the normal yellow ones, they are too easily identifiable and you could get kidnapped. There are some private services. I heard the one I took, Golden Tours, has connections with the CIA; they have been vetted and approved. Does the CIA work with them? I don't know.

Yesterday I had an information briefing. Basically about how to dodge or foresee potential ambush attacks or suicide bombers etc. It was kind of sad because a lot of it was videos taken from Convoys that had been attacked, videos taken from the Taliban or off sites where the Taliban was showing footage of their ambushes.

One video was a bit cool, a guy got shot, fell to the ground (but because of the bullet proof vest) got back up, fired and hid behind a truck. We were told he later outflanked the two shooters and killed them.

The bank machine at the base hasn't worked for five days. Most banks don't have an ATM. Welcome to Afghanistan. Finally tracked one down today and got some much needed moola.

The store I went to had an adorable girl selling chocolates or gum or something in front of it. I gave her 20 Afghanis (about 40 cents American) just for the hell of it. She and her little male friend or brother were chatting to me in Dari. I had no idea what she was saying. However, she did know how to say, "Please Mister, please, thank you" and "goodbye."

I have been told not to look at, talk or touch the women here ... sigh.

This includes the female children. So I was reasonably careful with this little cutie. In the countryside I will have to be extra careful because harmless behaviour by me could be

misconstrued and then some ass looking to redeem his honour will come hunting for my head. I have seen a few women or girls with makeup, no face cover and in some cases very little head cover. I guess they are pushing it. Most of them are covered up like ninjas. However with some, you can see a very nice shape, thus, leaving something to the imagination.

Sadly, Aysel and I are speaking now only if it's work-related. I am basically on my own outside the office. It didn't help that on a rare occasion she invited me to have dinner with her and Mustafa and I said no. I wasn't in the mood to socialize after her rather cold and silly behaviour. It got worse a few days later. As the two of them were leaving after work, I was standing on the main road near the entrance waiting for my taxi. She looked the other way and pretended not to see me and it was Mustafa who had to greet me. I could only shake my head. This sort of behaviour from her would seem to be ridiculous to any foreigner but if you have ever lived for any time in Turkey sadly, it's how some women behave once they have a man, like a damn ass.

On Tuesday it's off to Mazar-e-Sharif, meet the Commander, overnight there and then on to my post at Kunduz. I have been told we might have to sleep in a tent on the first night. But once it has a cot, I'm good.

Someone should theoretically meet me at MeS to facilitate a hand over at Kunduz, a fellow journalist, Heinz Graf, who has been doing the job in the North. However, he had to delay his trip due to road security concerns. So I can only hope to see him there.

I must buy a jacket tomorrow as it's starting to get chilly at night and winter is coming. The menu at my hotel was not so great. All Indian staff but no Indian food. Apparently, they have changed the menu due to the influx of NATO visitors.

I made a request for some Indian food and got it :-) a bit on the too hot side but a welcome change. HQ on the other hand, has a surprisingly good curry lamb and rice not T&T good but good enough.

Chapter 4

Welcome to Afghanistan and Get Used to It

Been a week now, still settling in at my post in Kunduz.

On Tuesday September 29, I finally headed off. The night before I was told that my 9 am flight would leave at 12:00 pm. I was very glad as this meant not having to arrive at the camp at 6 to get a security shuttle. I was told to come to HQ at 7 am to meet my "ride."

I arrived and got my bullet proof vest, helmet and luggage from the office. I had actually practiced putting on the vest the day before, so I wouldn't look like an ass in front of the soldiers. A well-armed American soldier from Missouri waited with me outside. I mentioned how polite all the soldiers were here and he said it was unlike any base he had ever been in. "Everybody is so nice to everybody, always saying hello."

The driver and a German soldier showed up. Everybody was armed to the teeth and had their vest on. I knew the driver and co-driver had to look out for possible insurgents so I kept quiet and let them do their job. It was like being in a movie as they kept a sharp eye on everything around them. The German sat in the back with me and was quiet as well.

About 25 odd minutes later we were at the airport. They shook our hands and took off. It was only then I realized the German was actually travelling on my flight.

It was about 7:30 and our check in was at 9 for a 12 pm flight. He then decided he would go in to check on the flight. He came out a bit confused that the flight was

departing at 12. Apparently, they had told him I was coming along but nobody told me about him. They told me about the delay but nobody had told him. Welcome to Afghanistan. His name is Alex.

I was on my way to Mazar-e-Sharif, his camp. I would overnight there and then on to Kunduz the next day. Hans a fellow FMTL (Forward Media Team Leader) would meet me in MeS and show me the ropes in Kunduz for a few days. Some Germans on the way home asked Alex if he would bump himself off the flight for a mate who was coming. Because their tour was over, he politely agreed. We had a chat and some donuts and coffee. While I was buying the coffee a Filipina looking girl asked me where I was from. I gave the standard reply - Canada. Because usually nobody here on this side of the world knows Trinidad and it's too much to explain every time. I asked her if she was Filipina and she said no that she was from India. I was so surprised. Of course there are Chinese people in India but still I was surprised. I explained that I was from

the West Indie and that I too am Indian. So, I guess we are bredren. :-)

Check in time and apparently my name wasn't on the manifest. The Germans' friend didn't show up so off went Alex but not me. I had to wait apparently even the standby passengers were being let on ahead of me. I made up my mind then and there to never leave my confirmation details to others. So I was bumped and told to check in at 11:40 for a 1:35 pm departure. The German guy coordinating everything was nice enough to help with my bags and point out the coffee shop. I had a meal set my alarm and showed up at 11:35 only to find out they had changed the check in time to 12:40 and we would leave at 2:30. Welcome to Afghanistan and get used to it. At times like these I must remember the size of my paycheck and just breathe.

Finally made it onto the manifest and into the departure lounge. I then had a 20-minute nap. I admired the way these solders can just curl up and go to sleep. Two American Filipinos sat opposite me. One of them had a real cool deadly look á la Jet Li. I was surrounded by soldiers of all nationalities. Finally I got on the damn plane. The usual big, green looking plane, I still couldn't figure out the seat belt. I sat opposite some Indian lady who was on the flight and had been smiling at me since the departure lounge. Thirty minutes later we were in MeS. I was told someone would be there to greet me but saw no one. I walked up to the PAX desk which helps with all problems - turns out my guy Hans was there asking for me.

The MeS Camp is huge about 4000 people mostly soldiers most of them German. It is just gravel and buildings however because it's big, the facilities are good, e.g., restaurant, gym etc.

The Print Chief - Christoph met us. Showed me around the PSYOPS Office and gave me a place in his room, the top bunk. When was the last time I had slept in a top bunk? The guy was so decent he even made up my bed for me. I noticed one thing right away. The German female soldiers are way better looking than the American version. Most of them look damn good. The USA has simply got to step up their game. Had dinner and a good night's sleep. Didn't stay up late on the net this time. I slept for about ten hours. Was paranoid as hell I would fall of the top bunk. I tried to say as close to the wall as possible. Before going to sleep, I had a nice chat in the yard with Hans and the other Germans. I mentioned my paranoia about the upper bunk. They mentioned that in the last year at least three soldiers had to be sent home because they rolled off the top bunk and seriously hurt their heads. Part of me laughed at the thought of them returning home from war early and explaining, "I rolled of my bed and hit my head."

But in reality, this was no joke.

The next day it was off to Kunduz, nothing would be complete if our flight wasn't delayed and sure enough it was by one hour.

However, finally at around 2:30 pm we were on our way. We arrived at a fucking dilapidated building. I was trying to understand what this hillbilly looking structure had to do with us. I asked if it had been hit with mortar shells. I was told, no, that this airport was actually run by the Afghan govt and NATO was being allowed to use it. We stood up in a hall had our names confirmed and then hopped on to some kind of armoured jeep.

I was a bit nervous because I knew that in Kunduz outside the camp anything could happen. However, about 10 minutes later we had finally arrived at the camp where I should be working for the next year.

Chapter 5

Finding a Room and Tolerating a Belgian Dick

Wednesday October 14, 2009

Well been here for a little more than two weeks now. Slowly trying to get a routine going and meeting new challenges as time goes by.

After we arrived, had to find sleeping quarters. Had to walk about 200 metres with my bags, thank God Hans was here to help. We opened the door to my office and found a young lady and man enjoying a meal for two. Thank God it was Hans who opened the door or I would've thought I had entered the wrong office. I had forgotten that my office which was once just ours was now to be shared.

Apparently, it had been empty for three months. Aysel had actually been here for a year. However, when given the promotion earlier that year she had to leave. Occasionally, the two local reporters would come in and even less occasionally we would have a fellow FMTL come and spend a week there.

When Hans came by in July to keep it going for a week, everybody converged on him when he unlocked the door. They have eleven hundred people in a 400-man camp and space is at a premium. They then made it clear that they would be taking over the office. Hans had to talk them down and they agreed to let us to share it. Thus six weeks later ... TADDAA!!! ... there I was!

I can understand why they don't take the FMT Department seriously, an office unused for three months and when I arrived, my side of it is covered in dust.

I made a pledge to be there as much as possible to make sure we don't lose it altogether. The female soldier with whom I share the office, Marie, is quite sweet.

She was worried about how I would fit in with all these Germans and soldiers and I don't even speak the language. She told Hans that I should tell her if I had any problems and she would do her best to help me. She claims that her English isn't good. She actually understands everything but can't articulate herself that well. She has never taken umbrage that I share the office and that she and her boyfriend, a Belgian soldier (the fellow we met with her on the first day), can't have the privacy that they used to. He on other hand, who I shall refer to as Belgian dick as I don't know his name, seems to be perturbed at my presence. However, the last time I checked, he has an office next door, which he shares, this is the Bomb Disposal Unit operated by the Belgians. He has walked out of the office once or twice in huff apparently peeved at the lack of privacy for the two of them. You can see that Marie is affected by it and feels helpless. I feel sorry for her but "dick" has to understand he is in someone else's office.

I saw him in my second week in the line at the canteen. Everyone here greets each other when walking by and if you know someone you automatically say hello. As he was behind me in the line, I looked at him just to greet, he looked right past me with a stoic expression on his face. Fuck him! Now I am really going to enjoy occupying that office.

I have no room. HQ told me that the camp would provide and the camp said they only provide for soldiers. After a lot of chat about how overcrowded the camp was, we got a tent. One hour to tell us and another hour just to tell where it was. The tent is big and built for eight. There was only one person in it and he left the next day.

Sharing a tent means putting up with other people's idiosyncrasies. The guy in the tent actually snored and spoke in his sleep at the same time. I didn't think this was humanly possible. I just got up and looked at him. However, the next day he was gone and it was just Hans and I for the next few days. Hans in addition to snoring occasionally in his sleep also sometimes groans erotically. Again this is not something I am used to. The first time I just sat up in my bed and looked at him. You just try to ignore it and sleep. However, one night I did have to bang on the wardrobe and interrupt his snoring.

Looks like I won't get my own room for quite a while. They have ordered it. Basically this is some kind of portable and on a good day I am looking at three weeks to obtain it and probably two to three months for delivery. Thank God the tent is big like twice the size of a master bedroom and it has AC and heat. However, I just sleep there. It doesn't really entice me in a homely manner. It's also quite close to the bathrooms and showers so I appreciate that.

I don't know much about camps but this one looks pretty big. If you are from Trinidad, think of the Queen's Park Savannah, if not, it's about 50 football fields or more. It's a large dusty looking place. The damn sand is everywhere but we are not that far away from the desert. There are a lot of brown or grey buildings usually surrounded by grey concrete walls. Not extremely picturesque but then again this is an army camp. They have planted lawns around the buildings. And what does stand out are the rose bushes. The roses are huge, about half the size of the average man's hand and they are beautifully red.

These people are going to have to get used to a brown guy who works here and is not an Afghan. The local staff are sent home at the end of the day but seeing me walk around in jeans or a pair of shorts, you can see them wondering just who the hell I am. During my first week I bought some lunch at the canteen and decided I wanted to carry it to the office. I asked for it to go and they just gave me a plate of rice and stewed beef in an open plate. I asked for it to be covered, so they put another plate on top of it. I had to ask for a bag which they did give. As the plate was not sealed, I put my hands on the top and bottom to avoid spillage as I walked. Just as I left the canteen, and with swirling dust all around me, I saw about three tanks about 80 metres away. They stopped dead in their tracks and just looked at me.

I knew what they were thinking, brown guy with a concealed package walking towards them. I was worried that the tanks would blow my ass to kingdom come. I figured if I acted panicked or suspiciously, that might evoke a reaction from them. So I did my best to continue walking and look as non-threatening as possible. They stood their ground and just looked at me. I just continued walking doing my best impression of a safe, unassuming individual. Some German fellow was coming my way on a bicycle. Realizing the situation, he looked at me and then just waved them on. They continued and as they passed me, I just glanced at them and continued walking straight as if passing a neighbour on my way from the supermarket.

Welcome to Kunduz you brown bitch.

At first all the buildings in the camp looked the same. At night there is usually a moon and in the first week there was a full moon. There are very few lights at night so that a rocket attack will be more difficult for the insurgents (We don't call them Taliban in NATO, we say "insurgents"). Getting around is easy. However, with no moon and very few lights, you better have a flashlight; you can barely see five feet in front of you. It's a shock when people just appear walking in the opposite direction, saying hello. One night around 2 am thinking I was familiar with the route, I started to daydream and found myself on a dead-end road. I tried to walk back and somehow found my tent. The next day I looked at the way I had walked and realised that I had no clue coming back and was just damn lucky to find my way.

It was really nice to have Hans around. He has been doing the job for about two years. He is a slim, medium height, blond fellow, handsome and ex German Navy. I really don't know many folks here and he was good company. Also I would have suffered in a major way trying to settle in without him Surprisingly most of these people don't' seem to know about our department. The fact that I am one of the very few coloured people in this camp doesn't help. Hans finally left about five days after we arrived. So now I am really on my own. However, the Friday after I arrived, we met the Afghan reporters I'll work with. They then came the next day and brought us some home cooked food. It was quite tasty. We invited some of the office staff, however, all but one declined, a Colonel who upon knowing that I worked in Turkey made sure to tell me what great leaders they were. I think the others were afraid of the effect the food would have on their stomach. This was understandable. I had the mildest of effects the next day. :-)

There is one army canteen, a store and a bar. The bar is called Lumerland. I usually just refer to it as "Lumberland," as it's easier to remember. I am not far off as translated into English it means lumber country. When the bar is closed there is nowhere to go. However, they have a pool and beach volleyball court. I did go for a swim and appreciated looking at the ladies in their bikinis, an unexpected thrill in this part of the world. I had thought I would be stared at being the only brown guy at the pool but they seemed to control themselves. I understand the Germans like to go topless when at the pool but here in the army I think they have been advised not to.

During my first week, Hans and Aysel mentioned how crazed the soldiers can become around a woman. Despite only being here for six months (four for the Germans), they are very affected being in a mainly male environment. It's normal for women in a PRT to be outnumbered 50-1 or even more. These women get A LOT of attention. The bonus out of this is that the mediocre looking ones who perhaps were not that appealing at home now become mini celebrities. In many cases they pick and choose their men at their leisure. Some gladly look forward to a return tour just to enjoy the prestige they would not normally get at home.

They do have a big, useful gym and it's great to have access to one again after all these years.

Because of the cafeteria hours, I always eat dinner before 7:30 pm. No late-night meals and I have lost some weight.

Surprisingly although this camp has some noise, it doesn't seem to be as noisy as downtown Istanbul :-) so I don't have any problems sleeping.

Made some friends with the Filipino and Kenyan Kitchen staff, very nice guys and of course they speak English so we enjoy speaking to each other. The Kenyans actually know TT because of the World Cup in Germany.

One night I came back to the tent around 1 am and discovered someone had taken the extension cord for my electric cable. I wasn't about to wake up guys with guns to ask them if they had taken it. It's not like I could do anything about it. There were some new soldiers and

I figured it was them but with more than one tent I didn't know who. I just laughed because they knew someone was using the tent and took it anyway. I don't use the tent much so I wasn't too bothered. My plan was to just get one the next day. However, when I woke up, I saw an empty tent and just grabbed the extension. Problem solved.

I told Marie about my problem and asked her to write a note in German so that I could attach it to the chord. She practically went bonkers.

"What!! Do you want me to go and speak to them!!" she said rising out of her chair.

I made it clear that it wasn't necessary, I just wanted a note.

Her initial note was something like "Don't fucking touch this" but in German. I told her that it would be my backup and that to just say it politely with no profanity. In the end I never bothered to use the note, I just hid the chord in my clothes when it wasn't being used.

Regarding Marie, she's an attractive woman about 168 centimetres tall, nice strong, looking legs and ass and shoulder length, black hair. Many male soldiers find reasons to come in and ask her questions during the day. One American soldier even tried to use "German lessons," as a reason to meet her. He didn't get very far.

Thursday Oct. 15 2009

We had a party tonight. BBQ and free beer. I don't' think this was Oktoberfest but who gives a damn. If you are a beer lover then this was heaven. Everywhere you looked soldiers were walking with armfuls of beer.

There was live music. It wasn't too bad considering they aren't professionals. There was also some kind of fire dancing, fire eating guy. I had a good time with the Filipinos and Kenyans. We chatted and enjoyed the beer. I don't give a damn about beer but free alcohol is still appreciated.

I met some other Germans as well and we all had a great time chatting, listening to the music and drinking in front of Lumerland. There must have been 50 men for every woman.

Chapter 6

"Do You Work in the Kitchen?"

November 7, 2009

Well it's been over two weeks since my last entry quite a bit has happened since then.

I am slowly getting to know my reporters better Sayed and Hamid. I was given a debriefing about them when in Kabul. Steffi, a pretty, blonde German had the post for a year before Aysel so both debriefed me. Steffi now works in a different department within CJPOTF. Both she and Aysel practically had the same thing to say. Regarding Sayed, keep an eye on him. He seems to think he is the leader there especially when the FMTL is not around. He should be double checked when having to confirm any expenses. It's not uncommon for some Afghan workers here to try to scam their employers if they can. As they put it Hamid is the sweet one, really down to earth and friendly. Sayed handles print matters and Hamid, radio reports.

On Sunday, October 25, I was invited by my reporters to go Hamid's home for lunch. It turns out we had to stop at a press conference first.

Some local residents, including many ex-militia had gathered to agree that they would no longer pay a tax to the Taliban. This is a harvest tax that is stated in the Quran. But really it has nothing to do with the Taliban. As I looked out at the thirty odd men in their flowing beards and turbans sitting in the hot sun, they looked like harmless, old, Muslim men. However, the term "harmless," would be the least correct to describe them. Many of them are ex Mujahideen. These men fought the Russians for years and survived. Perhaps a bit more bad ass than the average thug from North America.

However instead of going to lunch at Hamid's house, we were offered food after the Press Conference. So I sat with the reporters and ate.

I was immediately a little wary. As foreigners we just can't eat Afghan food, it has an effect on our stomach. The meal was fine, shish kebab, salad, rice with meat. Everyone sat on the carpet with their legs crossed, which after a while started to affect my circulation. I think Sayed realized this and offered me an elevated position (carpets) next to him. But I tried to be a man and tough it out.

I realized that a lot of them were eating from the same plate. I made sure to eat only from my half of the plate. I don't know if the guy next to me picked up on it but he let me have my own plate. I think they pampered me a little because I am a foreigner. The meal was quite tasty and there was Pepsi to boot. ☺

They decided not to go to Hamid's house as we had already eaten. Also I wanted to be home at about 3 pm because I was still cautious about being out too late. Thank God, I look the way I do, at first glance everybody thought I was Afghan. It was a great opportunity to meet the local reporters and have a chat with them. We then went to a place to have some tea and chat. It was nice enough looking. My reporters know the Manager and he invited us into his office to have tea with him and his friends. We conversed for a while and looked at some satellite TV. They were looking at an Indian movie.

We eventually left after an hour. Kunduz city doesn't seem like much. A lot of the streets are dusty and worn. The central area looks better of course. However, this city and the country in general have suffered some kind of war or another for the last 30 years. Thus, a lot of the beauty has just been destroyed. If you are lucky enough to leave the city and see the rural areas, the beauty is simply breathtaking. This was once a country renowned for its beauty and was so popular with tourists. That stopped once they embraced Communism and the Russians stepped in. It will be a long while before the glory days of Afghanistan return once again.

Twenty-four hours later, I felt the effects of the food. I went to bed with an upset stomach that night. I had a slight feeling of wanting to throw up. I just kept thinking of dry brown bread. The next day I felt worse because I had a headache. However, at the end of the third day I felt better. Strangely enough at that very time the local staff in our block invited us to a dinner. It was right in our block. I was worried about the repercussions. However, I was told by one of the locals that the Chef was used on base so it should be ok. Great meal again and watermelon for dessert. I was very full and absolutely no side effects the next day :-)

The following Thursday night we had an earthquake, really, about 1 am Friday morning or so. I was watching a movie in my office (because I have the net there and I still sleep in a damn tent). I noticed my chair shaking but I thought it was my legs shaking so I kept trying to adjust my them. Then about 20 seconds later, the desk and laptop started to shake. I ran out into the corridor and by that time it had subsided. There was only one other person in the office block so we chatted about it. He said the shaking had been going on for a minute. Apparently, there had also been another earthquake about a week before, however, I never felt it.

One of my Filipino friends, James was leaving on November 6. So I really enjoyed spending the last week chatting with him. He has an ability to make friends with everybody despite how quiet he is. So through him I was having great chats with the Belgians and Germans, sitting late into the night, drinking and exchanging anecdotes. I call James "Mr. Congeniality."

As we exchanged stories, one that caught my attention was what they had to say about the local Chaplin. Max, a tall, bald, handsome, German soldier explained that the Chaplin and members of his religious group would have late night get togethers in the chapel. In a sarcastic, romantic voice, he told us, "They put on the nice romantic music and light the candles and hold each other close and dance, yah."

Everyone laughed.

I looked at him. "But it's a church."

"Yes and they hold each other in the candlelight and dance very close, yah.

I couldn't understand how a priest could participate in such acts in a chapel.

I must admit the Belgians seem quite nice. There are three groups of Europeans besides the Germans, the Belgians, Dutch and Swedes; they are all quite nice and friendly when you get to know them.

I only knew James for three weeks but really got to like him and will miss our late-night conversations.

The Germans and even some of the other soldiers or foreign civilians seem to be rather unused to a coloured man who is not an Afghan working amongst them. With the Afghans there is a certain protocol, e.g., being checked when entering or exiting the camp, and restricted admittance to certain areas like the showers, pub and certain high security buildings. Regarding the security check when entering the camp, I have to argue that those with my ID don't get searched. They just ignore me and go through my stuff anyway. This is something I am going to have to get used to.

A lot of them do a head jerk when they see me walking by. I get a quizzical look or have often been asked "Do you work in the kitchen?"

When I explain that I don't, they look at me in a confused manner, "You don't work in the kitchen?"

Sometimes, I get a little fed up. I ask them "Do you work in the kitchen?"

"No."

"Have you ever seen me in the kitchen?"

"No."

"No. I don't work in the kitchen."

Some of the showers are communal. For those not acquainted with the term, it means both males and females can use them. There is a changing room and then you walk into another room with about eight showers and a bench. Each shower has a curtain. Most of the Germans don't give a damn and just walk around that room naked. I have made jokes with some of the soldiers about what could happen if we were to meet a female in the communal showers. I actually kinda freaked when one walked in.

The communal shower I usually use was under some renovation. So they told us showerwise to use another one from November 1-9. I figured no problem, I just walked over to the other building and showered. After showering, I went into the adjoining room where the sinks are and started to shave. Sometime later, a woman (who works in the Canteen) walked in. I jumped figuring that I had been using the women's shower. She explained to me that it was no problem as this was a "coed shower."

I felt a bit like a pervert who had invaded sacred territory.

"I don't' usually come in here," I explained in a hurried, panicked voice. "But my shower is being renovated."

She just smiled at me and walked into the shower area. I decided to finish shaving as fast as possible. I had been very relaxed in that shower assuming it was all men. I have since showered very carefully making sure my curtain doesn't move too much. Every time there's someone showering with the curtain open a bit, of course it's a man. Also, some guys just dry off in the centre of the shower room without a care. I am going to assume that perhaps they know when the women come. Or with these Germans it's just no big deal. However, I have never again seen a woman in that particular shower.

Strangely enough back in my regular shower two weeks later. (Actually, I don't have a designated shower but this one is in the residence area closest to my office), I had finished up and was tying my shoelaces, getting ready to exit. I could feel someone behind me not moving. I looked around and saw a gorgeous, brunette German girl, her long, brown hair halfway down her back. She was wrapped in only a towel which covered the lower half of her breasts and went about a third down her legs. As I looked at her, she said "Hello."

I responded," Hello," making sure to visually take in the sight of her to the max without ogling and seeming perverted. I then turned around, finished tying my shoes, picked up my bags and bade her goodbye.

She never moved, her eyes fixed on me.

I thought her behaviour strange and then realized she must have thought I was an Afghan and how was I going to react to the sight of her.

I must admit that as a man of any nationality in a war camp, I was rather cool in my handling of the matter.

Chapter 7

I Am Not a Refugee and a Door Is Not a Window

November 19, 2009

Around November 3, the rep for the American State Dept. at the Camp went with me for a drink at the bar.

We stepped outside and had a chat with a group of Belgians, very friendly and funny. One German joined us, a bald, thickset fellow who started chatting with us. We were laughing and having a good time, after about half an hour he asked me "So you work for the kitchen?" Indicative of how few brown people work for ISAF at this camp.

I smiled, patted him on the shoulder and explained "No, PSYOPS," and he just blushed.

We had a great time talking football, women and other things. At one point he mentioned that a girl in Germany wanted only to be his "fuck friend." I explained I had first heard the term back in the mid-nineties and had taken great pleasure in the discovery. It was a pleasant night of 'man talk."

That night an officer came up to me and said I had to vacate my tent by November 18. I asked where I would go and his answer was he didn't know. I repeated myself and explained we worked for the same organisation.

He could only tell me he would get back to me. I just laughed because otherwise I would've been angry. I later went back to the office drunk and explained to my bosses at HQ that I am not a refugee and that these people have to treat me with some respect.

Aysel and Steffi never had this problem because in general women are treated with kid gloves wherever they stay with ISAF/NATO in Afghanistan.

It's been five weeks in a damn tent! Some Americans had shared a tent with me

a few days before and were surprised at this. When given a tour of the offices, they recognized me when they entered mine. They explained to the German officer, "He's been in a tent for five weeks." They guy just looked at the floor and then explained

some soldiers have been in a tent for six months.

Not in my area they haven't. There are loads of empty tents.

Well it turns out that the camp has been growing faster than they can keep up. They are building additional rooms but that will take a while and in the meantime, we have to just improvise. It does not help that I am not a German citizen, I have no boss here and they just don't give a fuck! However, I do have an office at ISAF HQ and they should have been on this in terms of acquiring my container.

Karl, the Chief Forward Media Team Leader, AKA the ass, said he had sent in the application for one to be sent to me but in actuality he hadn't.

They told me that it would take about two months to arrive. They suggested that when I came to Kabul a few days later that our Commander would speak to the new PSYOPS Commander for the North and he could make a call for me. I was really angry with my Chief for being so dumb and telling me the container would come in December. However, Aysel, the Deputy Chief is back from her holiday and maybe now there will be less ineptitude.

On November 10, I was off to Kabul for a conference. It took two planes to get there. Once I got to the military airport in Kabul there was no shuttle service for another 8 hours and the idiots weren't answering their phone. Thank God I had a few bags. I got a shuttle to the main gate and then called a taxi. However, people very new to Kabul wouldn't know about these things.

I dropped off my stuff in the office and went for lunch. I then joined the conference afterwards.

Of course I had met Hans but now I would meet the other eight FTMLs who were scattered throughout the country.

I had been given a minor heads up about them when I arrived by Aysel.

There was Michael from Manchester, a handsome fellow about 172 centimetres in good shape with blondish, brown hair. Aysel made it clear. "This guy is friendly and charming and very eager to get ahead."

Lisa from Canada was an army brat, growing up on bases in Canada and Europe. She seems to be in her mid-forties and has done a helluva job in her province. Not only has she been good at providing stories but she has worked with women in the area on different social programs to the point where a street in the town has been named after her.

Maurice is ex American Army. His wife and stepdaughter live in Belgium. He's a funny guy, always cracking jokes.

Allan is from Canada and ex-Army. He is located in Kandahar.

Imran is from Pakistan but now lives in England and once worked with the BBC providing his talents in one of his languages which I believe is Pashtun.

Adrian is a former Romanian Captain and was briefly in KDZ keeping the office going for a few weeks prior to my arrival.

There is Jake, a former TV reporter from Toronto and finally Katherine, also from Canada. You get the impression Katherine does not have much longer left with us. She is based in MeS. Like many civilians who have come to Afghanistan for the long term, she has found adjusting to life in a camp somewhat difficult. I don't know all the details but she has been late with her reports and has been a bit sullen when spoken to on the phone. She was going to receive a good talking to and a letter of warning when she arrived for the conference. However, she probably had a decent idea of what was imminent and opted out of it, citing "illness."

She has simply prolonged the inevitable.

We all met for dinner at an Italian restaurant that night. The dinner was ok by Kabul standards. It was great to have a lot of English folks to speak to. They asked me a lot of questions about TT. We also talked cricket and football. :-)

The conference lasted three days, I didn't listen to much of it. I get the impression a lot of soldiers were only half awake as I was. However, there was some useful info on how to spot a potential bomb, e.g., a van leaning too heavy at the back probably indicated a bomb or an X painted on a vehicle which would be a signal to the locals to stay away as it was a probable explosive.

What I will never forget was the video of the Taliban beheading their prisoners. It was normal during their regime to publicly behead people on live TV for such deviance as watching TV, singing and dancing.

The video we saw was of an Italian journalist who had been captured along with his minder and driver on March 5, 2007. The minder is the one who organizes your logistics and meeting contacts.

Both men were Afghan. The Taliban had asked for a ransom for all three or they would be executed. The government negotiated for the Italian but not for the locals as the general policy was not to negotiate with terrorists. Naturally, the public vehemently voiced their disapproval. The excuse offered by the Prime Minister was that the Italians were spending a lot of money in the country in terms of defence and infrastructure. The two Afghans were beheaded and the video disseminated by the insurgents.

What got me was the manner in which it was done. They didn't just do a quick swipe and cut off the head. The held each man down and slowly cut off his neck as if slicing a block of cheese to make a sandwich.

The minder never moved and his head was deposited on his corpse. The driver struggled like crazy. He was held down by three men while the fourth performed the decapitation. His head was then also placed on his body. The insurgents then began shaking hands and slapping each other's palms in obvious celebration of their accomplishment.

I mentioned to a soldier how strange it was that the minder never budged during what had to be a terrifying experience. He pointed out that sometimes the fear just paralyzes you.

My heart broke for those two men. It made me acutely aware of man's inhumanity to each other.

I saw an email reminding me of Safety Training for Saturday and Sunday. I figured this had to be a mistake because I was due to leave on Saturday so I erased it. However, on Thursday at the office, they mentioned it to me. Typical ISAF communication. Anyway that meant two more days in Kabul for me so no problem. Imran and I went to an Indian restaurant. I have also been ordering a lot of Indian food from our restaurant at the hotel. The restaurant Manager has taken a liking to me so if I order a large meal, he charges me for a small. He noticed me reading the Biography of Brian Lara, the cricketer. Like a lot of foreigners he is quite impressed that I went to school with Brian and know him a bit.

Later that week, as I was enjoying a coffee, he came up to me, "Sir, I wonder if I could ask you a favour."

I found myself wondering what favour I could do for him.

"If I can. What is it?"

"When you go home for Christmas if you meet Brian Lara, could you get his autograph for me?"

I couldn't help but laugh. I hadn't seen that coming. "Well if I see Brian, I will make sure and ask. He's very nice so I am sure he'll say yes."

No. I never saw Brian.

The hotel is the Heetal which I stayed in during September. It is run by Indians but I think they are a bit amateurish at this business.

The room given to me had two glass doors and no curtains. It was a huge room with a minute carpet so although there was heat, the floor was damn cold. There was also no hot water in the shower. Because of the lack of curtains, people could see right into your room. I walked outside to see if others had a similar problem. They did and seemed less perturbed about it than I. One woman was watching TV on her bed. In another room, a man was brushing his teeth in the bathroom wearing only his underwear. I made sure to complain and they told me they would deal with it.

By the end of the second day I just lost it. Apparently, despite my complaints they had covered the windows but not the door. Therefore, people could stare right through the glass door into your room. I really lost it because of no hot water.

They immediately gave me another room. Again there was a window at the top half of the door and no curtain. I was going to have to spend yet another night with passers-by looking directly into my bedroom. This time I went nuts again.

I walked into the reception area and started shouting at the only person there, some poor fellow who did not speak much English and obviously had no real authority.

"I am paying one hundred and thirty-two dollars a night and I can't get a curtain for my room after two nights," I shouted.

"Yes Sir. Sorry Sir," stuttered the receptionist.

I walked over to a curtain in the room. I held it, "This is a curtain!!!" I then raised the curtain away from the window, "This is NOT a curtain!!!" pointing to the windowpane. I repeated myself twice.

All the time the poor fellow just kept apologizing for something that wasn't his fault. "Yes Sir. Sorry Sir."

I had not lost my temper like that in years. I walked back to my room and once I had calmed down, I felt really badly for shouting at someone who had nothing to do with the problem. It turns out that earlier that night Imran had also shouted at him for not having access to hot water for two days. Poor fellow, he really did have a bad night.

The next day when I came in, they had nailed thick pieces of cloth over the window, the room was quite dark.

I just started to laugh because how many days do I have to say "DOOR". As I explained "A DOOR is not a WINDOW!!" However, the technician was there and changed it quickly. That day they were late with my coffee, I decided to call them to see what was up, only to discover the room had no phone. :-)) Did I mention I was paying a $132.00 a night?

The training took place at the military airport covering areas such as personal injury, as well as basic security. It really was just a repeat of other basic training in terms of how to spot possible bombs etc.

The co-ordinator AJ was a cool guy, who works in the Civilian Personnel Office. He gave Imran and I a ride every day and even helped me book my ticket on the military flight when nobody at the office would answer me about the booking.

I spent the night at HQ, I figured I might as well save some money. The good thing is we get an extra bursary for being away from the office so the extra days here aren't so bad. I get additional money and a chance to enjoy the city. However, I was anxious to get back as I was worried the Germans would have taken down my tent already.

I realize that when you work with people not everyone is going to be your buddy. However, I think the simple concept of a greeting when you see each other should not be a problem.

I had noticed during the conference that if I saw Allan in passing at HQ, he would try to look away but as we were passing shoulder to shoulder, he felt compelled to make eye contact. I would nod and so would he. However, when at the airport, a number of us stood just outside the departure lounge waiting for our imminent flight. This was a different part of the airport for a higher security domestic service. I saw Allan and he had a trapped look like it was too late to look away. I nodded and so did he. He then turned away and started chatting. Twenty minutes later, he and his group walked off to his flight. He never even looked back to say goodbye. I thus concluded that Allan was a dick.

I met a nice French civilian woman on the plane. She works in our city and we've seen each other quite often at the base. She's short, petite, probably in her middle to late thirties with ash white hair. Not surprisingly she is quite popular with the German soldiers. She's not bad looking but here I think a woman's hotness becomes tripled because of the predominantly male environment.

She works for the Water supply company for the province and invited me to a press conference the next day.

I arrived and found my tent still there. There were two Americans in it, one who had been there two weeks before with his friends. The other was an Afghan who lives in the USA. They will be here for a year and like me need a room. Like me they also had to leave the tent the next day.

We were told of our new tent. Unfortunately, we are sharing it with a lot of Belgians. I am now in a more crowded tent. I only hope these guys are transient. It's obvious no room is coming soon. The soldier who was supposed to help said he would, now he doesn't answer the phone.

I think the office will just have to send a container. The Americans are complaining a lot but it's their first week. I've been at this camp for six. I think non-German soldiers are just not a priority in a crowded camp. There are probably empty rooms somewhere but no one wants to tell us. The next few months will be interesting for me.

The Press Conference at the water company was great. I met a lot of foreigners, got a tour of the Press facility and ate some great Afghan food.

I went to the showers near my new tent and later found out I had mistakenly used the showers reserved only for women. However no one came in when I was there so it worked out ok.

As I work for ISAF, we have been told our intel is for anyone who works for the organization. However, I have noticed that the Americans like to pump you for information but at times can be deliberately vague if you ask them a question, e.g., they will be talking about an incident that happened with an Afghan soldier.

"Where was this?"

You will then get a blank look.

"Oh. It was somewhere.

I try not to be offended as I know they are simply following orders.

The American in my tent, Jim, is a huge guy. He's about 6'7", a lean 235 pound with receding light brown hair. The Afghan, Sayeed, actually lived in Canada during the 1970s before moving to the USA. He is in his early sixties but looks at least 10 years younger. I enjoy having a coffee with them after dinner as there just aren't that many people for me to socialize with.

Today is my birthday, I will do my best to make something of it. I have had quiet birthdays before but this one may break some records. ;-)

Chapter 8

Happy Birthday to Me and Scantily Clad During Winter

November 19 was my birthday and it wasn't so bad considering my location.

The day was relatively quiet. However, that night I made myself go to the bar.

I was determined to make the best of it. I showered, put on a nice T-shirt to go with my standard jeans and made sure to slap on some cologne (something I usually never do in the camp) before exiting the tent. The Belgians were looking at me curiously and one of them asked me "Are you going out?"

I looked at him quizzically, "Out?"

"Yes, are you going out somewhere?"

"No, not really. I am just going to Lumerland."

The other Belgians just laughed.

I met the American State Department Rep there, he introduced me to some Germans and we spent the night getting drunk and chatting. It's amazing how everybody can get along with some alcohol in them. :-)

On Sunday, November 22, the reporters brought some local food. I invited the Americans from my tent and two Germans, including one I got really friendly with at the bar. The food was great as usual. Unfortunately, I got ill for a day as is the norm when I eat Afghan food from outside of the camp.

Some time in November, I found out that my brother's cousin, (we have different mothers) an ex-Miss Trinidad & Tobago was involved in a sex tape scandal. Within 24 hours the tapes were emailed to me. Even in Afghanistan you know Trini people's business. However, I quickly understood this was not standard porn but rather some ass technician fixing her computer, discovering a private video and uploading it to the internet. I shut off the video and quickly deleted it. I can only hope someone dealt with that fellow in the appropriate manner.

In late November I heard a sort of gushing sound in my office. I looked around wondering what it could be. I looked at the climate control and saw this blue liquid streaming out. There seemed to be no way to stop it. One of the officers ran to call the technicians. However, for the next five minutes I was mopping water out of the office at an alarming rate. Thank God there's a garden outside of my office, so the water had somewhere to go.

The repairmen came and apparently fixed it. One of them said he would look around to see if there were any problems because of the water. That was around 4 pm. He never came back. His tools were there so I really thought he would. At 8 pm I turned on the heat because I was cold. At 11 pm I left. The next day when I returned his tools were gone. Amazingly a week later two guys turned up to fix it and were surprised that it was already repaired. I was a little shocked at this lack of organization, after all, these are Germans, renowned for their coordination and logistics. However, the soldiers quickly explained don't expect the same thing in the German camp in Afghanistan.

During winter, I have found myself too lazy to actually put on a bunch of clothes to go to the porta potty which is about 25 odd metres from the tent. I put on a jacket or sometimes just walk out in a T-shirt and boxer shorts. The temperature is around minus five degrees Celsius. It sounds like a crazy thing to do but when you come from Toronto, a brief walk in minus five ain't no big thing.

Well my dumbness caught up with me. I got really ill on Saturday December 5. I was in bed for the most part of the next two days with a fever and headache. I was still a bit ill three days later. However, I managed to get some work done.

I have just found out we are paying 600 dollars for a driver but I have never seen one. My reporters have their own car and whenever I travel, they drive me. They brought some guy who they say is a Driver and he gave me a copy of some Afghan ID which he signed. However, I think this is a scam so next month we may cancel his contract.

Despite my illness being over, three weeks later, I can't shake the cough. I look forward to the arrival of my container in January.

Chapter 9

Boom!! And a Gift from God

December 2009

I left my Camp on December 13 to ensure I would catch my flight from Kabul on December 18.

This was my Christmas leave and I did not want any obstacles. For the first time ever, I bought my tickets online rather than from an agent's office.

I had to leave Kunduz early because flights were regularly getting cancelled for reasons such as rain. The runway where we are isn't the greatest and apart from the

military planes some of the commercial planes have the odd problem.

There was no way I was going to miss my Christmas holiday, so I paid for my own flight (30 Euros) and got to Kabul early. I was flown on a domestic service, Pamir Airways. The plane was very small with propellers. I hadn't flown in such a plane since I was a kid. The army planes have propellers but they are much bigger.

Sayed my Print reporter picked me up. The plane was supposed to depart at 9:30 but arrived at about 9:25. First they let the women board and then had the men line up and eventually we went on. We left around 10 am. There was not toilet and no seatbelt. The latter really had me worried. I figured when landing we would naturally be leaning forward and wondered what the hell would happen at high velocity. They did however have an attendant who served us water.

We saw some beautiful green countryside and hills on the way to Kabul. Afghanistan is really a beautiful country but 30 years of war has really desecrated the cities. I decided to stay at the Heetal Hotel instead of HQ. I would have a better room and food there.

That decision almost cost me my life.

Two days later on Tuesday, December 15, I started to get ready to go to HQ. As I wasn't very busy and nobody really missed me, I had decided to go in at around 10 am or so.

I called my taxi as usual. I decided not to wait outside as I usually did for two reasons (i) it was cold and (ii) They are usually late because of traffic or some other reason. In the past if waiting, I would speak to the security guard on the road. He seemed very youthful, about 16 but I figured there was no way they would give a gun to someone so young to stand guard. He would try to chat with me. He was speaking Dari but with my basic Turkish, I could pick up a few words. It was funny as he would point out a cat or my clothes and I would understand the odd word.

However, on this day I decided to wait at the reception office. I wasn't going to waste a half an hour of my life in this bitter cold standing on the road. I went to reception a little before 9:45 am and asked one of the managers to get me change for a fifty. He left the office to walk outside over to Accounting. I heard a BOOM!! and the doors just flew across the room, with every window shattering. I just allowed myself to keel to one side on the couch. I was on my left side, covered in glass. I first ascertained that I was alive. I had experienced a bomb in Istanbul some years before but never anything this close and personal. I ran my hand down my face and side to see if there was any blood. I then checked to see if I was missing a limb. Thank God the windows were some kind of plexiglass. There was not a scratch on me. Had the windows been regular glass Lord knows what would have happened to my face.

I was sure the bomb was just outside. My first reaction was to dive under the desk. However, the desk was upright and there was a big space beneath it, not much protection there. I realized there was the possibility of a second bomb or gunmen coming in. The assistant in the room seemed more scared than me.

I took a peek outside and to my shock there was no burning car in the car park. I couldn't understand how the blast had done so much damage but there was no explosion to be seen. I then decided to run to the back of the hotel where the bungalows and restaurant were. Still thinking the Taliban could be coming in, I was a bit panicked. However, at that point some of the staff told us the blast had actually happened about 100 metres down the road. Realizing that we were not the targets calmed me down. I then called the office to let them know that I would be late. Aysel said someone would call me and tell me what to do. I thought "cool, they are coming to rescue me" :-) But nobody ever called.

I went downstairs to a bomb shelter with a bunch of guests and others who were about to start a conference. They then decided a little later that they would do their conference in the shelter. I thought no way was I getting stuck with them for the next few hours. Once we ascertained that the army was outside and that we were no longer in danger, I went back to my room. Fortunately, the internet was still working. In about an hour and a half they started cleaning up the place. Every room had shattered windows, many had broken doors. The car bonnet had flown about a hundred metres and landed on the hotel grounds. There were bits of tyre rubber all over the lawn.

The target had been the guest house of the brother of an ex PM. That house and the one across from it were basically destroyed.

The young security guard who was standing where I usually wait for the taxi was dead. In all about 14 people were killed. The next day about fifty feet from where he stood guard and in front of the Reception's door, I saw them shovelling his hand, limbs and other body parts into a garbage bag. It broke my heart. He never knew what hit him. The other guard who was standing in front of the gate and had a wall to shield him had his stomach ripped open by the blast. We wouldn't see him for three months.

However, I could not stop thinking about the young fellow, his life ahead of him and everything just gone. I thought about how I usually stood next to him and what would have happened to me had I not changed my routine that day.

I realized I had been given a gift from God. For the next few days I prayed for myself and that young security guard whose name I never learnt. I prayed for him to be in a good place and to find peace. I have never forgotten him. And every year, I reflect on him occasionally hoping he was in the Paradise that Muslims often refer to. I would also think how old he would be and of the family he might have had.

The taxi service did call about two hours after the blast to see if I was ok. The driver knew my routine and was wondering if I had been outside. He himself had been about 150 metres away when the blast took place. Had he been one minute earlier, we both would have died. I'll never complain about their late service again.

My office finally called me four hours after the fact to inform me that because I hadn't told them that I was staying at a hotel nobody knew where I was. Therefore, had I been injured or killed by the bomb I wouldn't have been covered by insurance. Strangely they never thought to ask me where I was staying when I had arrived.

Some of the hotel staff were still shaken up. The restaurant manager explained that because many of them were from Nepal or India their passports were being held by management. If they wished to go home, they were told to wait because there was a shortage of staff. They are working in a war zone and they have not been provided with life insurance. He is from India and we get along well. I made it clear to him that it was illegal for anybody to withhold his passport and that he could always complain to the Indian embassy. Most of the guests had cleared out after the bomb. The staff would be having a meeting with the Chairman of the Board on the Friday after the bomb - December 18, the day I was leaving. The Restaurant. Manager made it clear that if it wasn't a productive meeting, he was out of there. When I returned in January, I was told that he had left two days after the meeting. I felt kind of sad that I hadn't a chance to say goodbye to him. He was a decent fellow working hard abroad, trying to provide for his family.

My bosses didn't seem too concerned that I had just escaped a bomb; however, many other people in my department were. Every day they kept asking me how I was. I was basically ignored by my own superiors.

The day I left Afghanistan to go to Canada was one of the worst airport experiences of my life. I had been told to get there at the time of check in. If you get in earlier, they make you wait outside. My check in time was 8:15. I arrived at 7:45. It took ten minutes to get to the point to offload my bags. It took another 30 minutes to enter with the bags as they were checking everyone. It then took about ten minutes to get to the terminal entrance where there was a line. It was about 8:25 and I figured if I entered in 30 minutes, I would be ok. Well the line moved slowly and was getting longer. All of a sudden, I saw a bunch of people go to the front and make a new line. I checked and apparently, we were told that people for my airline Safi Air, should go there. I was relieved, it looked like we would make it. Well the guy who told us to form that line never came back and security guard at the front told us we would have to go to the back of the line. The Germans in my line went crazy and said no way. I figured what ever happened I wasn't alone. There was no order as everybody was pushing everybody trying to get ahead. I felt sorry for the people with kids. I myself had three bags so it was hell holding them and pushing. At some point I pushed past the guard as he stepped forward, I simply went behind him. I got to check in at 9:20. They then put up a sign saying the flight was delayed. If they had done this earlier, there wouldn't have been a riot.

Check in took at least 30 minutes and we had to argue with a few Afghans who thought they could cut our line. I was getting some serious TT flashbacks from my youth. A bunch of Afghans simply walked to the halfway point of the line and tried to slowly insert themselves. I was way at the back and I figured they could not possible be doing what I thought they were. I assumed maybe there was a desk up there or something. However, some Germans behind me went nuts. Three of them ran up to the gentlemen and in a not very subtle manner made it very clear that they should haul ass to the back of the line.

There was no TV telling us what time the flights were leaving so you basically had to ask. The immigration officer couldn't understand that I had a Visa exemption in addition, he was confused as to why I had no entry stamp into Afghanistan. I tried to explain that I had entered the country on a NATO flight, thus, no stamp. He just didn't get it and held me back to wait on his boss. After about ten minutes he decided to "do me a favour" and let me go.

Apparently, people were boarding the plane right away. I had no idea. There was no TV or announcement being made. However, I saw one guy go through the doors to the plane and then I realized that nobody else from my check in was in the Departure Lounge. I simply dashed through the doors and entered the plane. Had I just sat there and waited these fools may have simply said nothing and left me. After two and a half hours of crap I was finally on the plane. I had never stressed or fought so much to get on a flight.

Chapter 10

"I Am Sleeping on My Desk"

January-February 2010

After arriving back from Canada around January 6, it was straight to the hotel.

I had been in transit in Frankfurt before I boarded my flight. After changing terminals, I was looking for my flight desk. I decided to leave my bags near some chairs instead of pushing them all over the place. I ended up walking further than I thought I would. I found the airline I needed and then when I came back to my bags, they were surrounded by four German police officers with guns. I ran up explaining that the bags were mine. I showed my passport and was instructed I shouldn't leave my belongings alone.

The Safi airline had no movie as usual (for an eight-hour flight); however, the seats were damn comfortable and I slept well. I also chatted with a nice Canadian guy who was on his way to work with the Canadian embassy.

Unfortunately, I forgot to turn off my phone and the battery was dead when I arrived at the Kabul airport. This meant I couldn't call the secure taxi service that I usually use. I instead had to use the yellow cabs which could be dangerous. However, with my brown skin and stubble I figured I could pull it off. After bartering on the price I was given a taxi. I spoke only Turkish in the cab and told the guy I was from Turkey.

The Afghans love the Turks. I believe one of the reasons is that for decades Turkey has been the model of a free, secular, Turkish republic rather than an ultraconservative Muslim state. Although many countries have problems in Afghanistan, Turkey isn't one of them. Their soldiers are left alone by the insurgents. I therefore, play the Turkish card when surrounded by strangers in the hope that should I come across the Taliban, they will not look upon me as kidnap meat.

The neighbourhood where my hotel was had more intense security since the bombing a few weeks earlier. The guards at the entrance wanted to stop the cab and check my bags however, I shouted and showed them my ID and they were cool. As I approached the hotel, I almost didn't recognise it. They had almost completed a huge, thick concrete wall around it and were getting ready to install a huge metal gate. The guards now were more anxious every time a car pulled up.

I checked in and told them that I would work from the hotel (sleep). Karl the ass, as I like to call him was still on leave and Aysel was cool with it.

About a week later I was back at the camp and it was life as normal. We were now in the height of winter and I still had no room. However, I was supposed to get a container at the end of January. Karl had wasted about two months of my time last year because he didn't give in the application regarding the container.

The two guys I had been sharing my tent with were still there. Jim had actually been replaced in November by another American, Bill. He was around 168 centimetres and about 200 pounds. He may have been a bit fat but if he had lost 25 odd pounds, he would still be a pretty solid guy. Along with his stout physique, he had short, brown hair and a similar coloured beard and moustache. He had been a police officer in Dallas. Like Jim he was secretive about what he did in Afghanistan. However, he did open up every once in a while.

It was Bill who gave me some insight into Afghan culture by explaining "Man on Thursday."

The Afghan weekend is Friday and Saturday. Therefore, their Thursday night is like an American's Friday night. They kick back and have fun.

Bill explained that some years back whilst he was training "Afghan Marines," they had drones that would pass over at night. They had the ability to see through the tents sort of like an X-ray. The soldiers would get a call from Command.

"What the fuck is going on down there?"

"What do you mean Sir?"

"There's sex going on in every tent down there."

"It's Man on Thursday Sir."

"What the hell does that mean!!??"

"Well, it's Thursday night sir. The men are relaxing."

It was not uncommon for the men if alone with each other for prolonged periods of time to simply become intimate with each other.

In early February, Bill and Sayeed got their own container and were off. We had suffered and complained in the cold together. But now I was alone and it sucked even more. The next few days in that tent were tough. It had begun to snow a lot. The snow was piling up on the roof. One night, I felt something wet on my face. It was a sort of dripping. Where the fuck is this coming from, I asked myself. Looking up, I realized it was snow leaking through the roof of the tent.

If I moved to another bed, I would have to take the sheets and make up the bed. I was too sleepy for that. I was also too sleepy to get up and physically move the bed away from the drip. So I just rolled over to my left. Problem temporarily solved.

We had a problem with the heaters, they would stop working at minus10 degrees Celsius. That's a very cold tent. So they put in heating tubes for all the tents which were attached to a generator outside.

On Monday February 8, my internet stopped working. That same night the heat stopped as well. The generator was blowing regular air through the tubes. No hot air, meant a damn cold tent. There was now mist in the tent. I had to think hard regarding where to sleep.

I momentarily thought of sleeping in the arcade/internet room. However, I realized that the soldiers would enter early in the morning so that wouldn't really work.

I opted for my office. So at 4 am with snow falling in minus 15 degrees Celsius, I walked the two hundred metres with my sheets around my shoulders and my pillow in a Foot Locker bag. I slept on the desk. It was uncomfortable but I figured out if you are tired enough you will sleep. I put two chairs next to the desk so I wouldn't roll off and break my neck.

I had been messaging and emailing Karl for a week about an update on the container. This time I was less subtle in request. Aysel was on leave. Adrian was there to assist Karl. So this time I CC'd him in the email. I knew it would embarrass Karl and be the impetus for a reaction as opposed to the usual shit.

I have been waiting six months for a container. No one has the manners to tell me when it's coming and I am now sleeping on my fucking desk.

If I can't get a proper response this week, I shall just take a flight, work next to you in your office and ISAF and get me a room at HQ.

I knew that there was no way Karl wanted me in the office with him and he would be uncomfortable that Adrian saw the email.

This shamelessly, incompetent dick told me that the Commander had shot down the idea of the container. No one had told me and I had wasted another two months waiting for accommodations that weren't coming.

Now I was given a story about a container that belongs to our department in the province of Takhar. The idea was someone would package it and have it shipped to me. This time I was told five weeks to go. So now I was sleeping in my office.

The mechanic showed me how to open up the generator and reboot it if it should fail to give hot air. This only worked sometimes but I got damn good at doing it late at night - in the dark, in sub-zero weather, flashlight in my mouth and my hands freezing like crazy because of the cold metal.

However, after about a week of it working on and off and me being paranoid every time I went to the tent at night, I just got a cot and moved into my office. Thank God I don't share it with anyone.

I had been spending a lot of time in my office before but now I was actually living there. Occasionally an officer would pass by, see the cot and just smile. As I am not German my plight is not their concern. It's hard to believe that we are all working for ISAF yet an ISAF employee can be ignored like this. Anyway they are building accommodations, until then it's the tents and whatever comes with it. In reality, I am not a soldier in a unit and not a priority. I tried to be understanding about this in the beginning but now I am in fucking awe at the lack of interest in my welfare, a citizen of a NATO country who is a human being like anyone else in the camp.

If I am not working, I am on the net surfing or looking out for the odd sport event via illegal feeds. I am at my office until well after midnight, looking at films or just trying to find a way to pass the time and have a life. I usually take some tinned fish from the canteen. The kitchen staff give me some bread and I make sandwiches in the office. I happen to have obtained some homemade pepper sauce from my aunt during my Christmas visit to Trinidad. I have no hesitation in saying she makes the best pepper sauce in the world, the whole wide world. Her sauce can make any meal just seem better and so it did with the sandwiches.

One night in February, I received a call from my mother, I stepped outside the office for a better reception and it seemed that the Lieutenant Colonel who was the new Chief Media Officer was having a barbeque with the other officers and the American Consul Representative who had an office in the same block. They looked at me and I could hear them murmur "We should invite Veersen." So they did.

They were barbequing steak, only steak, nothing else and they seemed to be eating it in copious amounts. I accepted their offer and then I remembered my aunt's pepper sauce. "You know," I said looking at them "… I should get my pepper sauce."

I dashed into my office and returned with my bottle. I explained to them what it was and that it had been homemade in Trinidad. I warned them to be careful as it was delicious but hot especially for the uninitiated. One soldier in particular was slapping it onto his steak. He couldn't speak English so through the Lt. Colonel, I suggested that he should be careful. Some of the soldiers then started pacing the corridor next to the garden, inhaling and exhaling attempting to get cool air into their mouths. "Does your aunt work for the insurgents?" asked a Captain in between gasps.

However, when I looked at the fellow who had taken generous amounts, he was absolutely fine and showing no signs of discomfort. "I am impressed," I said and smiled. The Lt. Colonel translated. He then explained that he was from East Germany and that they had a spicy mustard that was similar. I refused to believe that any mustard in East Germany could be as hot as my aunt's pepper sauce. I smiled and nodded. Regardless of what product they had in his country, as a rule white people outside of the Caribbean do not usually handle pepper sauce that well.

I finally had my first rocket attack around mid-February. Just the day before I had been marvelling at how there had been no rockets since my arrival five months earlier. The funny part is I never even heard it, I was watching TV in my office and had it not been for the alarm I would never have known. My area is considered secure so we were told just to stay there. However, I put on my helmet and vest just in case something came through the window.

After about an hour I forgot about it and continued watching my DVD.

I had gotten a bit fed up with Bill and Sayeed thinking they could pump me for information and then clamming up if I asked a question. There had been a conference at a local hotel in late 2009. The Governor and Mayor were going to be there along with a lot of high-ranking military. I asked the two of them if they were going and they said no.

"Really?" I said in surprise. "You're not going."

"No, we're not," they both answered shaking their head.

Imagine my surprise when arrived to see them both there and Sayeed being the official translator.

I understand these guys have their security concerns but I didn't like being played for a fool. I decided that the next time they thought they were getting information from me, I would deal with them.

Sure enough Sayeed was passing me in the corridor in January. We greeted each other and then he causally asked, "So anything new happening outside the camp?"

"Well, there's some stuff happening in Qala-I-Zal."

Qala-I-Zal was a damn dangerous place. It was located in the western part of Kunduz. The Taliban had their flag in the area and the local Afghan National Police or Afghan National Army (ANP/ANA) had limited influence.

He looked at me, "What stuff?"

"Well, about a hundred prostitutes form Uzbekistan have come to Qala-I-Zal. The Taliban have set up gambling there sort of like Las Vegas. Anyone is welcome and it's like a neutral zone, no gun play. You can have the women for the night for one hundred dollars. My reporters go regularly with their friends. They keep inviting me to come along."

Sayeed looked at me, his face a study of concentration. I could see he was making mental notes.

Now go tell that to your fucking Commander I said to myself as I walked off.

Chapter 11

Kunduz University and Piles of Shit

March-June 2010

As I was now sleeping in my office, I had to get used to being there 24 hours a day.

With my luck after a week the heat in the office stopped working. I got up at about 4 am one day just shivering. They fixed it but then it stopped working again a week later. By that time, the winter had subsided a bit so I just wore jeans and a sweater to sleep. You cannot imagine the words that were coming out of my mouth to describe Karl who had just wasted the last five months of my time.

Thank God I had some leave in March and went to Istanbul for about ten days. I had a good time relaxing and eating some good food.

Between February and late June I experienced about five rocket attacks. Usually if I am in the office and a DVD is on, I don't hear them just the rocket alarm afterwards.

However, on one occasion I was showering and shaving late at night. At about 1:30 am I heard a whistling sound. I said to myself that sounds like a rocket. You actually had time to think while you heard it coming. I felt reasonably safe as the shower had concrete walls and a lot of protection of other walls and corridors in the front. I just crouched down low next to the door. then all I heard was a big BANG!!!

Within ten seconds the alarm was on. Usually you are supposed to run or stay in the nearest available concrete building. And not leave until given permission. This could take more than an hour. However, we had about six attacks between January and June. Therefore, I knew the Taliban routine a bit. The second rocket usually comes in ten minutes or not at all. Usually there is no second rocket. I just decided to walk back to my office in my boxer shorts and T shirt in the pitch black of the night.

You could see the surprise on some of the soldiers' faces at around 1:30 am, as I just walked into our office area in my boxers and T Shirt.

One night a little after 1 am I was taking a walk. As I returned to the office and was about to close the door, I could hear a whistling sound. I opened the door and at that moment heard a loud BANG! Just 20 seconds earlier I had been walking in the vicinity of the explosion. These Taliban guys usually attack us before midnight, I guess such courtesies were no longer available.

Sayed and Hamid had made it clear more than once how uncomfortable they felt travelling on Pamir Airways. I really couldn't blame them. In early May during a Kunduz-Kabul run, the flight was forced to return after 30 minutes due to technical difficulties.

The following week, Pamir Airways 112 crashed into the mountains killing a reported 34 passengers and five crew on May 17. I thought of this plane and its no seatbelts. Not surprisingly, approximately a year later, the government shut them down.

We had been told by Command in Kabul to help out in the camp or local community in some way using what skills we had. I started part timing at the local University. I wanted to keep my teaching skills up and this was one way to reach out to the community.

They were quite eager to have a native speaker with experience free of charge.

Naturally, this was a different environment to previous classes in Canada, Colombia or Turkey.

You could see the women entering the University dressed like ninjas. Covered from head to toe.

I remember on the drive to the school, I would see some girls on the back of a local minibus. You would see some feet which is about as much as you ever saw.

However, once in the school the girls removed the Burka. They were still of course modestly dressed.

In the class all the females sat on one side of the class and the men on the other.

These were students in the Teachers Training Centre. I made it clear that I would mix them in groups for activities and they were agreeable with that.

I taught two classes. They were both very polite. They would get up when I entered and when it was time to leave. They would stand and not exit until I did. At first, I couldn't understand why they wouldn't leave and I kept telling them they could go.

I also developed a technique to recognise covered girls entering the school who were my students. I would watch the shoes and then watch the shoes again in my class. It was just a way to pass the time. One girl enjoyed flirting with me and actually shook my hand in front of everyone. You could get stoned to death for this in certain villages.

There was construction going at the University so some classes were not ready.

The toilet for the men was a disgusting place behind some trees. The facility was a building with individual stalls that had holes in the ground with shit piled pretty high. It was all over the floor about three inches high. I did my best to NEVER go there. But some students were at the dorm and had to use it. I thank God that I never went to a school like that. I ate nothing and tried to drink just a little water so I wouldn't have to urinate. However, that never worked and at some point, I had to. I would try to find the stall with the least pile of shit. There was an open space in the wall which I guess is a window. I tried to focus on the trees outside and just zoom in on a particular leaf on the tree, making myself as unaware of the moment as possible. Thankfully, a few months later the new buildings were ready and they had proper toilets. Would you believe once the new toilets were available, I never needed to use the facilities.

One thing a foreigner learns while living in Afghanistan is how seemingly unperturbed the locals are regarding bombings. One man's norm is another man's bizarre.

Teaching at the University one day, we were practicing "if" sentences, specifically " the zero conditional."

I would begin, "If there is no school, …"

"We study,"

"If the teacher doesn't come to class …"

"We study."

"If there is a bomb …"

"We study."

I looked at them in surprise. "Class! If there is a bomb …"

"We study."

My eyebrows furrowed a bit. "Guys! If there is a bomb …" This time I motioned with my hands as if mimicking the sound of an explosion.

Najibullah, one of the better students and an employee at the Kunduz PRT, looked at me, "Teacher, if there is a bomb," he looked out the window as if curious and then looked back at me, "we study."

I paused for a moment, considered what he had said and then responded, "I will accept that answer only in this country."

On another occasion, the Taliban had gas bombed a women's University opposite the Kunduz University. Most of the students had collapsed and ambulances had been sent to take them to the hospital. When the students informed me of what had happened, I became worried.

"Are we going home?"

"For what?" they asked.

"Well there was a gas bomb." I motioned in the direction of the incident. "Shouldn't we go home."

"No, it's ok."

"But the wind might blow the gas in this direction."

"Oh no. It's ok. You can teach."

And *that* is life in Afghanistan. ☺

I continued to sleep in the office. There was a gate near the office that someone had clicked the lock on but left it open, so every time the entered or exited, the lock would clang on the rest of the gate. It would drive me crazy.

I didn't feel comfortable walking around the office area in front of the officers in my sleeping clothes. So I would change in the office. In terms of using the toilet, I got some plastic cups and every morning, you could see me showering the roses in front of the office with bright yellow stuff from the cups. Those are some damn healthy roses now.

Karl took sick leave in early March. He was supposed to have gone for just two weeks; this evolved into four months.

I went on leave to New Delhi, India in late April. Four days after my arrival, Osama Bin Laden was killed by US troops in Abbottabad, Pakistan. When I heard the news on Indian TV, I remembered the words of my reporter, Sayed in Kunduz. He and Hamid had explained that most Afghans were sure that Pakistan wanted to sabotage the NATO efforts in Afghanistan. By doing so NATO would be forced to ask the Pakistani government for assistance as the two countries bordered each other.

It was back in October of 2009, "I guarantee you," said Sayed. "… When they find Osama bin Laden, they will find him in Pakistan. He is in Pakistan right now."

Regardless of Sayed's accusations against the Pakistan government, he was spot on as to where they would find Osama.

We had a conference at the end of May and it looked like the Commander did not want Karl to come back. Many of us believed that he deliberately wanted to get away because of the all the screwing up he had done. So in May he said he would resign and come back to hand over the reins to his successor. He was told by the Commander not to bother they would pack his things in a box and send it to him.

I was glad because I believed that finally we would have competent folks running the office. Hans and Michael covered shortly for Karl whilst he was away with Aysel doing most of the work as usual.

They were great in resolving problems with the container. At one point I had been told that they had to put an extra roof on it and that would delay them sending it. Then they told me that I should take care of it and they wouldn't send it until I had an assessment from a company. I thought this was rubbish of course I would get an assessment just send the damn container. I had already been waiting seven months. In hindsight they were probably just ensuring that the cost would not be some ridiculous price.

Hans spoke to the Commander who told them to send the container - problem solved.

With Karl, Lord knows how many more months that would've taken.

So in June, just before my July vacation, my container did arrive.

Now I just needed furniture for it.

One addition we have had to our team is Sammi. He is an Afghan-British fellow with a background in Media Management. He was sent to Kandahar to be the Forward Media Team Leader there. Having migrated from Afghanistan as a boy not surprisingly he is supposedly fluent in Dari

It did not take Aysel long to realize that he did not have the skills for the job. If given an assignment to edit and deliver, he would take close to a week whereas the rest of us could have it done in 24 hours. Aysel had a chat with a member of the editing staff and it was agreed that he would be let go within a month.

Chapter 12

How the Game is Played and Acrimonious Relations

July – September 2010

Whilst I was away on leave in July, I heard via email that Karl had come back. I couldn't believe it. WHY!!!????

He had been completely useless as a Forward Media Team Chief. I couldn't believe that he was so shameless. Actually, it turned out that I was wrong he was even more shameless than any of us could ever have imagined. The man didn't just come back. He actually got a promotion. He was now Media Chief. That's right the BOSS of everyone who had anything to do with Media. Turns out the new Commander and he had worked together in the past. The bitch made a call and presto - new job. Worse yet, it is illegal to offer a civilian this job as it must be filled by a member of the military, of which he is not.

Welcome to how the game is played. ☺

When I came back and informed the others in the other camps, they went ballistic, basically echoing my sentiments. Worse yet Aysel was on holiday and Karl made Sammi the FMT Chief. However, he changed the title to "FMT Co-ordinator." I asked him what was to be Aysel's role once she returned. He said that would be discussed with her. The appointment of Sammi was a complete and utter joke. He had the least experience as an FMT Leader and couldn't edit. He was lucky just to get the job of FMTL, now the least experienced guy was going to be our boss. He didn't even properly know the logistics or paperwork required. What Karl was trying to do was get people who knew the least about him because those who did, had no respect for him. With Sammi, this was just a puppet whom Karl would control and tell what to do. In other words Karl would still have a great say over the FMT.

Naturally Sammi was like a fish out of water trying to come to terms with paperwork and the normal routine of things and he was constantly referring to Karl. Some of our colleagues were so disgusted with Karl, they refused to answer the phone when he called.

Aysel and Sammi were now at the same level. However, the relationship between Karl and Aysel had become incredibly acrimonious.

When I had arrived the previous year, Aysel would mention what little work Karl actually did, usually reading the German newspapers online or just not answering emails. I didn't take it too seriously as I prefer to get to know people myself.

During the next few months and putting up with his wanting communication skills, I had become to realize that efficiency was not his middle name. As Aysel was his deputy many of us who had a problem with him would turn to her for an answer to our queries. By mid-November of 2009, she had gotten fed up. She made it clear to all the Team Leaders that she would no longer take complaints about him, she also informed Karl that she would no longer buffer for him and tell lies, from now on he would have to handle these problems himself.

Fast forward to June and with Karl out of the picture most of us were happy with the more efficient environment. However, once back, not only did he insult Aysel by basically having Sammi as her Co-Chief but he showed a petty side to himself which basically had his credibility diminish even less in our eyes if such a thing was even possible.

He would give Aysel reports to write which basically did not have much to do with her job. It would take her all day to do it. He would then return them the next day with corrections. This went on for weeks. She was unable to do any work due to these "duties."

Understandably, she was frantic and in despair. Whilst I was in the office on one occasion, I could hear Sammy telling her, "I wish the two of you could sort this problem out. It's not fair to you and I really wish you could solve the problem."

All I could think was you are the fucking FMT Co-ordinator. Why the fuck don't you do your job and go speak on her behalf rather than have her abused like this. However, this man was no real Co-ordinator or whatever the fuck title they had manufactured for him and was lucky to have the job he did.

After two weeks of this and no end in sight, Aysel went to the Commander in tears, frustrated and offering to resign. She was moved over to the Atmospherics Department. It would have been a crying shame for politics to result in her resignation and Karl's ascension.

I found myself wondering if Karl realized or cared how little the FMT staff respected him.

It was now August and my contract would have to be renewed in September I had to play nice because the money was too sweet. ☺

I made it clear to Sammi that as my contract expired on September 15, I needed some proper notice of whether or not it was being renewed, this would be the difference between a holiday and just returning home. Karl was supposed to send in the response by August 15. Although he was a bit late, he told me to go ahead and book my holiday, basically saying that I would be rehired. Sammi even made a subtle comment about the fact that there was a lot of time and they had other things to do. What I tried to express to this inexperienced fellow is that we are dealing with people who FUCK UP the simplest of things all the time. One person had gone on holiday – assuming that Karl had done his job, only to come back and find out the paperwork had never been given and that he was then absent without leave (AWOL), basically a reason for dismissal.

However, after two weeks of them assuring me it would be taken care of, I just stopped thinking. Sure enough I was in Kabul getting ready to go on leave and I got an email from Jess from the CPO, (who knew I was waiting for the official OK) telling me that they had never received my recommendation or a signed new contract. Naturally, I messaged Sammi and he had Karl take care of it ASAP.

Finally, I had a chance to get away from these people. Off to London and Paris.

Chapter 13

An Ass Kicking, Shouting at the DCOM and a Possible Rotation

October – December 2010

After my return from my Leave it was back to work at Kunduz.

Life had gotten better. I now had a room. I only had to wait 11 odd months for it. I am one of the few people in the camp with my own office. I am sure there is some bitterness about that. There is limited office and sleeping space here. I had been asked by one of the officers if I would like to move over to where the Belgians are so I could work with them as I sometimes share my Atmospherics with them. I made it clear that I don't really work with them that much and that it wouldn't make sense. They could have just told me to do so but I was told by Hans that the Germans are far too polite for that.

I could now sleep and work well. They had changed the company that served the food in the canteen. In October they also moved to the new Canteen building. The food had definitely improved. Not great but a higher level of crap.

This new company was bringing its staff from India. If people thought I was kitchen staff before what the hell were they going to think now? They had asked some of the present staff to stay. But basically, they were offering them half the pay and almost double the hours. So the Kenyans and Filipinos said no thanks. It will be strange seeing all the kitchen crew leave. Most of them have been here since I came and now they are leaving en masse. It feels a bit like the TV series Lost. You're on the island and everybody gets to leave but you.

I had noticed that when I returned to the Kunduz Camp, I was getting a lot of big, bright smiles from the soldiers. I had seen some friendly people before but not like this.

I didn't quite figure it out until the third day when I went into Lumerland to get a coffee. The staff there always knew me better than the other soldiers because their stay was for six months not four.

As I ordered my coffee the soldier behind the counter looked at me, "Sir, if it's alright, I would like to ask you a personal question."

"Sure, go ahead." I found myself wondering what was coming next.

"You say you are from Trinidad & Tobago and you live in Canada. But you are wearing an Arsenal football jacket?"

I could not help but smile, "That's the personal question?" I explained to him that growing up in TT there were no really big clubs to follow. Most of us usually supported a major club in England some others, clubs in Italy or Spain. Arsenal was my club.

He nodded his head. "Ok."

However, that Arsenal jacket did seem to break the ice with a lot of people. Go Gunners!

There was also a female German police officer I would speak to from time to time. I had seen her around, however, in the summer around August, I was having breakfast outside one Saturday when she asked if she could sit at my table.

She explained that she was there to train the female officers. We both then began to discuss the problems of Afghan men giving women equality or even acknowledging orders from a female officer.

She explained that on one occasion the Chief of Police for Kunduz had come to their training facility. He was introduced to the instructors and shook their hand. However, when introduced to her, he looked past her, ignored her outstretched hand and moved on.

We had an FMT meeting in October at HQ. Great chance to get away and get some decent food. Hans warned me that this would be an opportunity for Command to bash the FMTs. As he put it, "This is an opportunity for Command to give us an ass kicking."

He wasn't wrong.

Apparently, Karl, well aware of his days when he didn't work too hard decided to have a word with the Commander about how we worked.

We were shown better ways to edit, file photos and given some useful info from HR.

Perhaps some of these people knew that they should not be there and this was their way of humbling us. During one session Sammi pointed out the correct way to do the Atmospherics and then showed us examples from the different FMTs where it had been done incorrectly. What really pissed me off was that earlier that year the net in my office was not working. I had to use the net in the entertainment area of the camp and there was no option to download the template we use for Atmospherics. I explained this to Sammi and gave it to him using MS Word. He knew damn well the circumstances under which I had to do it but still used mine as an example of the wrong procedure. I found myself wondering if this was just his way of trying to look useful and competent.

It became obvious to me that nobody gave a fuck about our problems. The focus of this meeting was just to bash us.

At one point I tried to politely point out that Sammi was a little too inexperienced for the job and that perhaps it should have been offered to more experienced members. The response was we could apply for the job. If so, then why the hell wasn't it advertised months ago when they wanted to fill the position?

I also pointed out that Sammi had no idea what the procedure was and who to speak to when one of our reporters had been threatened by the Taliban. The Deputy Commander (DCOM) gave me some stupid response about whether or not I knew everything about my job. I didn't realize it at the time but when responding I actually shouted at him – which is not something you do. "Hey man!!," I started off and you do not speak that way to Command. "There are people being killed in their homes with their families made to watch. This is very serious and the protocol on how to handle this problem should be known. Our reporters don't have the luxury you do of living in a fort and being protected by armed guards." I felt Katherine grab my arm at the time. I didn't know why she was so concerned. However, later my colleagues explained that I had to control myself and not raise my voice at the Commanders. ☺

At that point I was thinking bye bye job. But I was told by others not to worry, it wouldn't come to that, plus these individuals would be gone in about six months.

Some of the people who work in the south where life is tougher and more dangerous hinted that they shouldn't be stuck there all the time and that there should be a rotation with the folks in the north. Naturally, those in the north, that being Katherine and I opposed the idea. I made it clear that I had gone through hell for my first year and finally when I had a room someone was going to come capitalize on this because they wanted to "rotate."

Katherine was even worse than me. She just kept going on and on about how she had developed contacts and done such a good job and that she should be allowed to continue her good work.

She continued to talk about it after the meeting driving everyone nuts. Lisa who was sharing a room with her just started dodging her. Katherine is a good woman with a good heart but she really does beat a point to death. I think she knew that Lisa was getting fed up so she went off in a corner of the hotel by herself and read – giving everyone a break.

I was really pissed at the idea of moving down south. Why the hell had I put up with that crap for a year? Why hadn't someone wanted to come up then? What was pissing me off is that Michael was making noise about coming up north just because he knew the German camps had beer and wine and he wanted the luxury of having a drink.

The Commander made it clear that there would be no rotation. However, some offices would close and people would have to move to another camp. He didn't say it but probably someone would lose a job.

Then two weeks after the conference, the jackass said there would be a rotation.

In September or so during my Leave they opened the new canteen, much bigger and nicer. The Filipino and Kenyan staff would leave at the end of October and an all-Indian staff had already arrived in early October to learn the ropes.

It was kind of sad to see all the old staff leave. Every time one of the long timers left, I felt like they had been set free but I still had time to serve.

I had to wait for ten weeks to go on my Christmas Leave. It wasn't that long but it felt that way. I couldn't understand why it felt so tedious. I had a room, a great office, the only person besides the Colonels with one. But I was feeling claustrophobic. The tedious lifestyle was just getting to me. Fortunately, this winter was amazingly warm in comparison to the year before, about 18-22 degrees Celsius in the day and about 7 degrees or so at night.

I was told that I would be going to Zabul in the south. However, when I asked the Commander about it, he said no decisions had yet been made. However, Gaby assured me the Commander had already told them who was going where. Typical shit.

So I was off to Thailand expecting to see Zabul at some point in the new year.

Bombing of a guest house just outside my hotel in Kabul, December 2009.

Kabul airport on my way to Kunduz, September 2009.

A journalism lunch after a press conference in Kunduz, October 2009.

On my way from Kunduz to Kabul, my transportation is in the background, November 2009.

Local farmers holding a press conference announcing their refusal to pay a tax to the
local Taliban, October 2009.

Private bus transportation, Kunduz, October 2009.

Germans don't really need a reason to drink lots of beer. Me and some of the kitchen staff with all the free beer we could drink, Kunduz, October 2009.

Local Bedouin receiving aid from ISAF, Lashkargah, 2011.

Chapter 14

Dental Surgery and on to Lashkargah

From December 2010 to January 2011, I was in Thailand, holidaying in Bangkok and Phuket.

Reluctantly I returned to Kabul on January 10. I had actually cracked a tooth whilst in Phuket and thought of staying back to have it "fixed." What this really meant was an extended holiday.

Anyway once I got back. I was supposed to leave a day later to go to Kunduz. Turns out my flight got cancelled. I now had to wait about three days for the next flight.

I was then told by someone that if I needed the tooth fixed. I could get sick leave and go out of country to do it. Turns out the NATO Dentists only do basic stuff and the crown I needed wasn't part of the service. So quicker than you could say "buy a ticket," I was on my way to Istanbul for at least a week. ☺

I was late to the airport because of bad weather. Due to snow and mist the taxi driver just couldn't get there on time. I however, got through the check points very quickly. I was in a long line, which then got turned into two lines and I was second. I thought "things are going well." I should have known better in a Kabul airport. After about ten minutes, I realized no one was getting served. At the 20 minute-mark, they told us we were delayed for an hour. I thought no big deal, I still have time to catch my connection in Dubai. Then an hour later they said four hours!!!

I started chatting with a Pakistani guy behind me, who was a businessman in Dubai. We killed a few hours talking and then sure enough a few hours later, the line started moving. The original flight was unable to land in Kabul due to the bad weather. They, therefore, needed time to get a plane ready at our end. Our original departure had been scheduled for 7:40 am, we left about 12 pm.

Naturally, I missed my connection in Dubai and had to wait about 12 hours for the next flight.

A little more than two weeks later I was back in Kabul. I was greeted with the news that I wouldn't be going to Zabul as previously told, instead now I would go to fucking Lashkargah, Helmand province.

Helmand is in the south, just north of Pakistan. It's a kill zone and the opium capital of the world, the British have a PRT there. No one wants to go there, with the added discouragement that you can't get a bed and will sleep in a tent with others. I just couldn't believe that these jackasses in Command, well aware of my struggles to get a bed in Kunduz, sleeping without a room for 11 months have decided that it is I of all people who should now fuck off to Helmand and be bedless again!!

You sometimes hear that this is Afghanistan and you are not here for comfort. However, it seems that I seem to be getting screwed more than anyone else in terms of accommodations. You don't hear no bitch now wanting to switch with me.

I had six weeks left before I had to move on. And I was pissed off for all six.

My last two weeks I made no effort to clean the office or container. I was just so angry, it was a bit unfair to Hans who was coming to replace me.

He ended up coming like three days late. I had to remain for almost an extra week due to flight cancellations. They guy at Helmand, Imran who I would replace, happened to be in Kabul in transit and was waiting for me. He just gave up and decided to meet me in Helmand.

Once I was in Kabul, I ended up spending about six days instead of three due to flight cancellations. On the second cancellation I was actually at the airport, bags checked, when they took five of us off the plane due to overbooking. We were pissed, however, they booked us on an emergency flight for the next day and assured us we'd be on it.

Whilst I was at HQ, the Civilian Personnel Office explained to me that they had not approved my move to Helmand and it was illegal. I had approached them to see how I could get out of it. However, they told me that although they would defend me if I didn't want to stay there, the Command could later come up with "reasons" to not extend my contract. It was a reality I had considered before and therefore, decided not to pursue this course of action. However, for monetary reasons I do want to extend the contract for a third and final year.

When I finally arrived at the Helmand PRT on March 6, Imran was there waiting for me. The two reporters Tayeba and Hadad had met me at the airport. Whilst driving, Hadad in the passenger seat kept looking back but often he was looking past me. I finally looked back too. He explained that he was making sure that the Taliban wasn't following us. I immediately perked up. They then showed me spots on the road where the Taliban had killed officers or civilians. I then started paying greater attention to my surroundings.

Imran was well organized and had the place ready to go. He showed me where the files were, introduced me to the relevant people and we checked our inventory.

Although Hadad and Tayeba were friendly to me, I think my inability to speak Pashto hindered our relationship. Hadad speaks a fair level of English but he's not someone I have a lot to say to. After the first week, we stopped eating lunch together and I think they wanted me to go by myself so they could visit Face Book and see their mail on the office computer. They don't usually have electricity in this town so forget about them having a reliable internet source. However, there is a media centre they can visit to do their work.

It turns out that Hadad's written English is fairly substandard for this job. He's supposed to write his articles in Pashto and then give an English translation. The maniac tried to give me a summary of his Pashto. Then I caught him lying saying that he didn't have time at home because of the lack of electricity in the province; they usually get about two days of electricity on a good day. Although this is true, we have given them laptops with batteries. He lied to me and said that the LPs had no batteries. I just kept repeating myself until he spoke the truth. I couldn't understand this laziness and basic lack of performance. I knew that Imran was a very careful and professional person. There's no way Hadad could've last five months with him. I spoke to Imran and it turns out that Hadad was not his first choice but Tayaba had worked with him at another job before and really argued for him. Imran didn't want any friction in the workplace with his first choice so he acceded which I think is nonsense. As Imran speaks Pashto, he had Hadad just write in Pashto and translated it himself because he was aware of his substandard English. I was shocked that he couldn't find quotation marks on the computer and didn't seem to know how to use full stops or commas.

I asked many times to use the virus checker at home for obvious reasons. He assured me he was but at this point I doubted almost everything that came out of his mouth. On one occasion I had a British soldier scan his USB in the office as they had a superior virus checker. He had over one thousand viruses on the USB. I could only shake me head. "So you scan your USB at home?" I asked with a withering look.

With the passing of every week I noticed that he started to come in later and later. I had no problem with him coming in a few hours late because most of his work was done outside and he only needed about 30-45 minutes with me. However, I decided to say nothing to see how far he would push it. Lunch started at 12 pm and usually I got out there at around 11:45 due to the line. I started leaving the office at 11:25 if he hadn't shown up as yet as to not arrive too late and slow me down from getting a good place in the line for the canteen.

One day I stuck around until 11:35 am, went to lunch and deliberately came back an hour later, as lunch finished at around 1 pm. This little bitch had put his file on my desktop, had lunch and left. I immediately wrote out a Letter of Warning, citing his substandard English, continuously not checking his work properly with a dictionary and of course his crap about giving me work without discussing it with me. I thought the embarrassment would sober him up but his idiocy would continue.

Chapter 15

"I Don't Give a Fuck" and No More Air India for me

April 2011

Around January, Sammi had been given the position of Print Editor for the local version of the paper.

This time they made sure to "advertise" the position before bypassing Imran who was the best qualified and giving it to Sammi.

I found it strange that Sammi would sometimes call me asking how to get in contact with Sayed. I later found out from Sayed that he was being asked to assist Sammi with English-Dari translations. "So what am I, a reporter or a translator?"

"You are whatever CJPOTF decides you are. If they say you are a reporter then you are. If they say you are a translator then you are that as well," was my response.

With hindsight I realized that Sammi had been given yet another job that he was not up to and therefore, needed Sayed's help. I had tried in the past not to have any ill feelings towards him, after all it wasn't his fault that Karl had given him a position he wasn't suited for. However, this was now twice in a row and my staff was being inconvenienced because of it.

One of the few respites I got in the camp was to watch the One Day World Cup of Cricket. It was amusing to see some of the Americans try to understand what was happening. It was just as impressive to see some Americans explaining the game to their colleagues and being correct.

I got some insight as to how the Afghans felt about the Pakistanis during this tournament. I sat next to some Afghans and they assumed I was Pakistani. I got some insight as to how the Afghans felt about the Pakistanis during this tournament. I sat next to some Afghans and they assumed I was Pakistani. I asked why and they responded that I looked like one. I pointed out my red, tattered West Indies jersey that I was proudly wearing and made it clear as to who my team was.

They then pointed out a group of Pakistanis to the right, in front of us. "We just want Pakistan to lose," they whispered.

Every time Pakistan lost a wicket, they would give exaggerated loud claps and cheer. The Pakistanis would look behind them in distaste. When the last wicket fell, the Afghans hooted and clapped again very loudly. The Pakistanis walked out glancing at them with the look you would give an overbearing child that won't shut up.

Sadly, my team was also kicked out of the World Cup. About two days after, I could seem some British soldiers staring at my jersey. An East Indian fellow, looked at me "You're done and dusted mate."

I thought to myself does this ass not understand that you support your team no matter what. Five years later when the WI hammered England in the final to win the TI-20 WC, I thought to myself now, that's "'Done and dusted mate.'"

In April we had our FMT conference. I personally didn't give a damn.

I had been basically ignored in Kunduz when it came to requests for proper accommodations and now, I am stuck in Helmand because some people wanted more comfortable surroundings. I would leave two weeks after the conference to go on leave (India). As we usually came into Kabul a week before departure to compensate for flight cancellation, theoretically with these cancellations I could be returning to camp when it was time to return to Kabul. Instead of wasting a possible week like this I asked to just stay in the capital but was denied.

On the first day I just went through the motions. There was Karl with his usual blah blah blah which no one really cared about. Michael was put in charge of organizing the conference as Sammi was away on leave.

On the second day I got "ill," texted them and turned off my phone.

When I got there the next day. Michael came up to me and asked if I had a note from the ISAF hospital. I said no. He wasn't amused and made a sarcastic comment about me "playing the game better than that" and walked off. I could understand his frustration, he was organizing the conference and it probably made him look a bit bad. However, I was fed up with the mismanagement so fuck them. This would come to a head later on.

I noticed that Michael was very quiet around me thereafter. There would be a BBQ that night and it was up to our department to organize it. I stuck around and when I showed up at just after 6 pm, the tables had already been set up. I now had to waste about an hour in the camp. I went to the café looked at some TV and then killed some time in the office. When I went back to the BBQ, it had started to drizzle and I helped those there move furniture inside the adjacent soldier lodgings. We put the tables and chairs in the corridor.

The BBQ was good as it usually is. I chatted with a few folks – strangely most of the people from my department weren't there. I left not too long after eating as I really didn't wish to be there.

The next day I made no effort to come in early as I had no specific work for anyone. I came in around 11 am, had brunch, went on the net and then went to the office. Hans and Michael were there. Michael asked me where I had been earlier in the day and why I had missed the morning huddle. I told him there was no reason to show up early and he just went ballistic, screaming that I had not done much and hadn't helped with the BBQ. It made no sense to trying to tell him that I had actually come to the BBQ and helped out with the furniture – he wasn't listening. He was screaming and shouting away that I was "on thin ice with Karl and the Commander." He must have been under the impression that I cared. I was surprised at his tone as all the Senior officers could hear him. I had no intention of shouting and looking stupid in front of them. Hans quietly exited the office. After Michael took a breath from shouting, I asked him if he had anything else to add. He said no and I said ok and left.

Fifteen minutes later he was calling me. I ignored the first three calls but at the fourth, I decided to pick up, it could have been important and work related. He wanted to buy me a coffee and apologize for his ranting.

He tried to explain to me why my attitude was negative and with the Karl and the Commander around how it could affect me. my response was "I don't give a fuck."

He was a bit shocked and explained that he was only trying to help. "Mate, I'm trying to help you keep your job."

"I don't give a fuck and if Karl or the Commander ask me, I'll tell them I don't' give a fuck."

I made it clear to him that my attitude had nothing to do with him but I had been basically ignored in Kunduz and just when things were coming together, I get shifted to another camp with a tent and almost no chance of ever getting a room. If those in authority couldn't get their act together, I had no intentions of taking them seriously. He gave me some lecture about perhaps I wasn't cut out for this job. However, he seems to have forgotten the times he was sleeping at the back of the room during certain conferences.

Anyway we parted on good terms. Michael is a good guy, he just takes himself a little too seriously.

I returned to my camp and a week later was back in Kabul, getting ready to go on Leave to New Delhi.

On the day that I got to the damn airport my flight had been cancelled and the fools at Air India not only didn't inform us but had no back up flight that day and wouldn't answer the phone. It turns out there was a strike by their employees in their home country. It is the norm to inform passengers of cancellations as well as to organize an alternative flight. None of this had been done by AI. I have a feeling that it was because Afghanistan was a small market and they just couldn't be bothered or perhaps it was sheer incompetence. I bought a ticket with Kam Air and left the next day. I did get my refund from Air India and I wrote them a letter letting them know about their lack of communication skills and that would be my last time with them.

Chapter 16

Farts, Bombs and Life in Afghanistan

May-September 2011

After I returned from India in mid-May it was just six weeks and then off to Toronto.

The weather in May was sweet not too hot or too cold, about 19 degrees, perfect for going outside.

I had slowly adapted to my new locale. Unlike Kunduz, this was a very small camp. We were practically sleeping on top of each other. At one end of the camp there was a helicopter pad and a huge track around it. Late at night, the last thing I would do is walk six laps or more for the sake of exercise and just to relax.

When I had first arrived the PSYOPS team there was about to leave and about a week later the Handover-Takeover (HOTO) commenced.

However, before the HOTO there was one matter I had to make clear. One of the Captains had a bad habit of having our guys go out and do work his Atmospherics team should have been doing. The Atmospherics team here has about six locals. They are not real journalists but rather local DJs who have had some training. Hadad and Tayeba had made it clear that it was not their job to do the duties of the British team. However, this fellow had basically told them it was. The first two times that I was there he got away with it because I was told it was "a scoop." This was no scoop but rather he trying to take advantage of our guys for stories that were minor and not at a provincial or national level. He was also using Hadad to do translations despite having his staff of six whose job it was to do that.

I spoke loudly to my reporters making sure that the staff present cold hear. "Do not do their work. Do your own. Those stories do not concern us. Hadad, if anyone asks you to do a translation, don't do it. You have your own deadlines to meet. That stuff does not concern CJPOTF. If anyone has a problem with that, tell them to speak to me." The soldiers looked in my direction. No one ever said anything and we never had that problem again.

There are usually six to seven people in the PSYOPS team that arrives. Captain Allan Greer was in charge of the new group. I got along well with the whole crew and most of my interactions were with Frank, who was also a Captain, Michelle a very pretty, short, blonde Corporal and Betty, also short and blonde but about 170 pounds. I was pretty sure you had to be in some kind of shape to be in the army but nevertheless there she was.

Around the second week a British NCO of Indian descent sat next to me one night and began asking questions about the activities of the insurgent in and out of Lashkargah. I realized he was trying to get info and he just kept going on and on. Finally after about five minutes I said to him "You know it might be better if you spoke to the Afghans. They probably know a bit more than me."

He looked at me quizzically, "Where are you from?"

"Canada." I knew what was coming next.

"Where are you from originally?"

"Trinidad & Tobago, the West Indies."

I could see the look on his face as if to say what have I just done with the last five minutes of my life?

He is brown and not Afghan but for some reason even with my ID on my chest, he assumed that I was.

Not too long after, I got ill. It's very easy in an environment like this to pick up a bug. Within 24 hours I had a headache, fever and diarrhoea. I immediately went to the clinic. They checked me out and then the nurse asked, "How firm is your stool?"

I pondered the question and then looked at her, "How firm is firm? Let's just say it's semi loose."

She told me that I would have to go overnight in the sick tent and to go get some belongings if I needed them. I left a note on my desk for the reporters and explained to the PSYOPS team why they wouldn't be seeing me for `a while.

I went into the tent which had quite a few Scotsmen in it and the odd Englishman. I took a bed at the very end, settled in with my pillow and had a book nearby in case I felt the need to read. It wasn't bad enough that we were ill but we were near a beach volleyball court. You had to continuously hear the ball banging into our tent. You gotta be fucking kidding me I thought to myself. It just got worse as the night progressed. I ate nothing. I had a terrible headache, fever and a bit of a stomach-ache.

At around 1 am I felt the need to throw up. I walked over to the bathrooms but never actually made it. Just in front of the door to the clinic, I threw up on the paved walking area. I breathed, tried to collect myself and then went to the bathroom to wash up. I informed the nurse at the desk who told me to just go back to the tent, she would sort out the problem.

Upon throwing up, I felt much better. The headache and stomach-ache had subsided so had the fever. I was now able to sleep and even felt good enough to eat the toast they gave us for breakfast along with some coffee.

Many of the patients were napping during the morning. I decided to read my book, *Whispering Death* , the autobiography of Michael Holding, the ex-Test cricketer. All of a sudden, one of the fellows woke up with a start, "I shite myself. I shite myself!!"

The other soldiers immediately started laughing and shouting to each other, "He shite himself!! He shite himself!!"

I was so embarrassed for the guy. I tried to look away and pretend not to notice what was happening. But how could not notice with the Scotsmen laughing their heads off.

He quickly exited the tent and headed for the bathroom. One of the guys followed him outside laughing and pointing to the unfortunate fellow told anyone passing by, "He shite himself!!"

Someone informed the clinic and a crew quickly came over, cleaned up the bed and changed the sheets. A middle-aged male nurse in a very sensitive tone then told the group of us, "Tell the lad he can go back to bed now."

What I did not know at the time is that this a pretty common experience for the soldiers when living in a PRT. Many of them don't mention it unless their friends admit it first. I am pleased to say I was able to avoid any such embarrassment during my three years in Afghanistan.

As the tent was mainly Scots, they chatted away in their own brand of dialect. I was pretty sure it was some form of English, however, it just sounded like a kind of whistling. I couldn't understand a word no matter how hard I listened.

The Doctor came in around 10 am with two nurses. He explained that the vomiting had emitted most of the virus, hence the reason I was feeling better. He therefore, allowed me to leave if I wished. I gathered my belongings and just before exiting shouted to the patients, "So long inmates! Get well soon!"

Everyone including the medical staff laughed. The Doctor looked at one of the patients and smiled, "That's a bit harsh isn't it?"

Not surprisingly, although I am wearing my ID, people find it easier just to assume I am Afghan than read what is on my chest. Like in any camp, no one uses the normal walking path all the time, if you can cut through behind the odd structure as a short cut, you do. Taking one of my shortcuts one day, a soldier stopped me. "We don't allow people to walk here."

I knew this was a load of shit as I had seen many soldiers use that path. I looked at him, "You don't allow people or people who aren't white?"

He was a bit taken aback. "Well where are you from?"

"As the ID clearly states, I am from Canada."

The obligatory "Where are you from originally?" question followed up, which I answered.

His tone immediately changed and became less authoritative, "Well what I meant is we don't like the Afghans walking here."

"Well I am not Afghan."

"Ok."

John, the old Afghan American guy who shared out tent was a bit of a pain in the ass. He thought he could do office work in the tent. According to him he was having "classified" conversations and didn't want the Afghan guys in the office to hear him. So we had the pleasure of his voice in the tent during the day along with his radio.

It meant if you liked to sleep in or have a midday snooze, good luck. He would have the light on all day, even if he left the tent it didn't occur to him to turn the light off. He was always worried about noise in the tent but no one made more noise than him. His desk was on the other side of the sheet that separated us so I could also hear his radio even if he had it low.

One day he started freaking about people farting in the tent. Although this might be a legitimate concern, when you have seven men in a tent this is going to happen – tough luck. One morning I had just woken up, I hadn't even washed my face yet and he was shouting at me that he was going to make a complaint about the farts. "Well make the fucking complaint!!" I shouted and walked off to the bathroom. I really didn't mean to be that rude to him but I had just fucking woken up and the first thing I see is him in my face shouting away about farts.

We never really spoke much to each other after that. He would make some sarcastic comments about the tent stinking but he's old and old people can be difficult sometimes. During the first few months you would hear the odd bomb outside, usually early in the morning while I was still sleeping around eight or nine. Sometimes the alarm would go off and you would have to put on your bullet proof vest, helmet and haul ass to one of the safe areas, usually a concrete building or shelter. Other times the alarm wouldn't go off and I would just continue to sleep realizing it was outside and that there was no imminent threat to the camp. It shows how I have adapted to life to some degree here, where I can hear a bomb, realize that some people have just died and just turn over and continue with my slumber unperturbed. This is life in Afghanistan.

Sometimes I don't even hear the bombs depending on their location. One day I came into the office around 10 or 11 am and I saw debris on my desk. I later realized it had come from the ceiling. Apparently, a suicide bomber had set off a bomb at the Police Training centre about 200 metres from the front of the camp. However, as my sleeping quarters were on the far side, I had heard nothing.

There is one saving grace in this camp and that is the food. It is simply marvellous. Kunduz's canteen served crap. The food at HQ's canteen is decent plus they have actual restaurants to augment it. However, the Helmand PRT's food is famous throughout the ISAF camps in Afghanistan. Run by the British, the majority of the kitchen staff is Sri Lankan. I was told before my arrival how wonderful the food would be and I shrugged off the information. How great could PRT food be? Man was I wrong!

On the first day that I stepped in, all I could see was amazing food on the left and to the right about thirty feet long. There were curry dishes, regular stews at least four different kinds of salads, ice cream, cookies and chocolate as well as soup. As the months have progressed, we sometimes have Thai night or maybe a Mexican theme. It is great. Lining up for lunch and dinner are some of the happiest times I have had in Afghanistan. I am usually in the first five in the line for lunch and I feel so blessed and happy.

The PSYOPS team I work with is a decent bunch. We don't socialize much but if I or my team have a problem, they support us and back us if they can.

In March Hans left much to the joy of most of us. He never should have had the position as it should've been held by a NATO officer to begin with. Adrian and usually one or two of my colleagues ran the show from HQ and we had none of the nonsense from the past. The new Commander, Colonel James was a seven foot American and he seemed like an agreeable, approachable person. He and the new Media Chief, Lt. Col. Schulz had met me at the Regional Command, Camp Leatherneck in Helmand Province, a very barren looking Marine Camp. The purpose was so the Commander could understand what it was like in the field and how to improve relations between the RCs and the ISAF HQ.

The Commander was informed of the dickheadedness we had had to experience in the past so he could have a better idea how to have a better running Forward Media Team. With the old Command we had heard rumours of the closing down of FMTs, thus, there were some who thought they would be out of a job. However, we were told that no such thing would happen in the near future and that although the odd FMT would be closed down, one or two new ones would be opened. As my area is the most dangerous place in Afghanistan and is the opium capital of the world, there was no chance of my FMT being closed – so my job was safe. ☺

Chapter 17

Another Bombing and Indirect Gun Fire

March-September 2011

In June, the weather started to get a bit warm.

As the month progressed, it got hotter and in July we were in full swing of the heat. I actually went on leave at the end of June and returned around July 23.

After the bombing at the Heetal Hotel, I actually couldn't book a room there anymore. I was able to book once and then told they needed confirmation from my office. I made it clear that on the day of the bombing, I was the *only* guest who didn't flee and leave the hotel. However, they seemed to have been booked up by an Australian company of some sort and were never too concerned about my patronage.

One hotel I stayed at from 2010 to early 2011 was the Hotel Intercontinental. It was up on a hill and you had to go through three layers of security and checks just to get in. It was a well-known place for the diplomats and government ministers.

A colleague recommended it so I decided to give it a try. This was a place that had seen better days. The décor and the ambiance seemed to indicate that its peak had been in the late seventies or early eighties.

Their pool was empty and the "gym" was a dilapidated building behind the hotel with some old rusty weights. Not surprisingly, no one ever seemed to use it. There was a huge dining room that seemed to serve the same food. Actually, this was what was served to me in most Afghan restaurants and functions, rice with raisins, lamb and salad. It was tasty but monotonous. As I usually ate lunch outside, I didn't mind the dinner too much.

As a lot of high-ranking Afghan officials lived in the hotel so did their children. Every time I stayed there, I was put on the second floor. Sometimes I could hear the kids running up and down the corridor playing. A few times they took it upon themselves to run off with my "Do not disturb" sign and play with it. On one occasion I called two of them over. There was a little girl of about six with my sign in her hand. I extended my hand for it and she extended hers and shook my hand. I politely pointed to the sign and put it back on the door. As I did not speak her language, I motioned with my hand that she was not to touch. I did it in a firm but polite manner. I didn't want to intimidate her as kids will be kids and she really didn't know that she was doing anything bad.

Around March of 2011 I started staying at cheaper options in Kabul. It was a move that saved my life. On June 28 just before I went on leave, there were a number of bombings and a mass shooting at the hotel. It was reported that the first bomb was on the second floor, the floor I usually stayed on. I could only shake my head. How much longer could I keep dodging the proverbial bullet. Although the actual number of deaths could not be confirmed, it was believed to be at least 21.

I was in shock that this could happen to perhaps the most fortified of all the hotels. You had to go through three checks by armoured guards. No one ever said it officially but the reasoning was it was impossible to get all of that artillery inside without the knowledge of someone and that there had been some inside help.

One place that I visited whilst waiting to go one leave was the Lebanese restaurant. Aysel seemed more down to earth now and with Mustafa not around she seemed more eager to chat. It was almost like old times with her. She mentioned casually that she was getting bored in her relationship. Looking at them, it wasn't hard to figure out who was the lucky one amongst the two of them. She, Imran, Sammi and I went for dinner to the Lebanese restaurant, Taverna du Liban. I mentioned to the guys that because of Aysel we would get the usual complimentary dishes so wait for that before ordering. The restaurant had been banned from serving alcohol to locals. However, as Aysel put it, if the Chief of Police or a Minister said they wanted a beer you couldn't really do much about it. Then they were just banned from serving alcohol period. They owner solved this problem by just serving the alcohol in coffee cups so no one could see what you were drinking.

The owner, Kamal, came over more than once to have a friendly chat with us. We left after a few hours thanking him for his hospitality. It was the last time I ever visited the establishment. Approximately two and a half years later in mid-January, 2014, the Taliban bombed and stormed Taverna du Liban. Kamal picked up a gun and with his security tried to defend his restaurant. He was shot and killed.

Kamal and his restaurant were much loved by the expat community. It was a place where you could go and relax. In addition, you were always greeted and checked up on by the sociable and amiable owner. His death saddened many of us when we heard about it. Such was life in Kabul.

Aysel and Mustafa left us in April. They were off to Turkey. She had mentioned in the past about perhaps opening a bed and breakfast in the south of the country. She and I never spoke after her departure. However, through Facebook, I saw that they were married a year later. When I returned to Istanbul in March, 2013, I messaged her about meeting for a coffee. She never answered me. I was a little sorry to lose her friendship we had gotten along so well until she started her relationship with Mustafa. However, some Turkish women can me a bit strange with male friends once they get a man in their life.

My next leave was scheduled for late June. The days were usually around 35-40 degrees Celsius. This was not so bad as the previous year I had experienced as high as 55 degrees in Kunduz. I had thought the south would be hotter but I guess I was wrong.

I arrived at HQ in late June off to Canada for three weeks. At times in both Kunduz and HQ I didn't always wear my ID as I saw many civilians not doing so. I usually kept it in my pocket or under my jacket. There was a Belgian in our department who dealt with the bank payments of the locals. Dealing with him was a surprising pain in the ass. You would try to ask him a question. "I am busy. Come back later," and he would abruptly turn his back on you.

On one occasion I had asked someone in our office about a late payment for our driver. When he saw me, he said "You asked someone else about your employee's payment. If you do that again I will not help you. Speak to me and only me."

"Well you weren't around. I was in Helmand."

"If you do it again, I won't help you."

"I'm pretty sure it's your job to help me."

"Well I won't."

"Well if you don't, you can explain yourself to the Commander. You can tell him why you won't do your job." And with that I turned away.

I was a bit surprised by his behaviour because until that moment every Belgian I had ever met was so nice and friendly.

Here I was in June walking out of the CJPOTF building as he walked in.

He looked at me in a stern manner, "Who are you?"

"I have been here for two years, you don't know who the fuck I am."

His head jerked back. "Well you don't have any ID on."

"You've seen me walking around here for two fucking years and you don't know who I am." I pulled out the ID flashed it in front of his face and walked off.

Of course, I should have been wearing the ID but no one stops the white people not wearing theirs. Different rules when you are brown.

In late July, I came to the office to see debris on my desk. I couldn't understand what the hell had happened. It turns out the local Police Training Centre had a suicide bomber out front. As they were a few hundred metres away from us, we feel the effect sometimes. Because I had been sleeping at the far side of the camp, I didn't even know about it.

On August 7 at night, we suddenly heard a hail of seriously loud gun fire and what sounded like RPGs just outside the camp. The British soldiers and I jumped up and were naturally concerned. The Afghan guys looked towards the noise and then nonchalantly went back to work. We just looked at them and couldn't understand their casual nature. One of the soldiers asked them what was going on. Their response was "Indirect."

"What the Hell does that mean?"

"It means we are not the target, it's across the road," that being the local Police Head Quarters.

I pointed out to them that we are the enemy and we are always the target. All the insurgents had to do was turn around and fire our way. I never could understand why we seemed to be spared on a regular basis.

I opened the door a little bit and peeped outside towards the wall in the direction of the gunfire. The locals just laughed at me and made some comments. Although it was in Pashto, I figured it was something like "Look at the foreign guy, how he's freaking."

After about ten minutes, Captain Greer told us to put on our kit and go to the concrete shelter. My vest was in the tent, so I put on my helmet and we spent about 20 minutes with everyone else in the shelter. This was a classic case of being careless and stupid in a war zone. Because there was usually no action of any kind within the camp, I usually didn't bother to walk with my vest to the office in the Afghan heat. Had something more serious happened to us that night, I could have needlessly been injured.

We finally got a new FMT Chief. He was the ex TAA (Target Audience Analysis) Chief, who left and has come back a year later. His name is Errol Sloan. The position had been left vacant for about five months, as Sammi decided to become Print Editor for the local version of the paper. We are still confused as to what "editing" skills he's supposed to have. However, those in Command obviously have plans for him. And it was important that whilst Karl was there, he have people around him who didn't know about his basic incompetence and could tolerate him.

Hans and Lisa both applied for the position and it was a shame that they didn't get it. They are both quite qualified and whilst Hans subbed in that position, he did a great job. Again I'm sure Karl had something to do with this. After a few months Lisa withdrew her name. I'm guessing she was insulted that they were unsure about her, despite her excellent work and dedication since assuming the job.

Chapter 18

A Firing, a Transexual and So Be It

October-December 2011

When I came back from Leave in October, I no longer had to put up with that useless Print reporter, Hadad. I had been told a few months earlier that rather than fire him and put up with his protestations and the paperwork that would go with it, just wait for his contract to end on October 1 and it wouldn't be renewed. I wrote a very stern report on him which I forgot he would see ☺. It turns out he wrote a letter of protest about me. ☺

He said that I usually came in at 11 am, went to sleep at lunch time and looked at cricket on the net at night. The last part took me half a day to figure out as his written English was so bad.

Errol didn't really seem to care but told me that they had to show it to me. I explained that Hadad couldn't possibly know what time I came in as he usually chose to arrive at 11 even when I would ask him to please come in an hour earlier. I usually let him and Tayeba have the desk after lunch so they could browse the net. There were times I didn't as I had my own work to do and told them they could only use the net if it was work related. I made it clear to Errol that nighttime was my time and I could do what the hell I wanted on the net. I didn't bother to tell Hadad, as I wanted to finish on a good note. It was truly amazing how he pushed it and seemed to assume that I would just tolerate him.

We were supposed to have a conference in a few weeks. My flight got delayed, so Errol said there was no point going and returning in a short space of time especially as more flights would probably be cancelled. It was would be logical and more expedient to just stay in Kabul and go back to Helmand after the conference.

We would stay and have the conference at Green Acres, a reasonably decent fortified hotel in Kabul. They had a bar and a pool so we were all looking forward to it. We had two new additions to the PSYOPS team: Bess, a Print Trainer from the US and Samanta, a Radio Trainer from Latvia via England. I had met Bess before my Leave and Samanta after I came back.

Whilst I was away, we had fully moved the office from ISAF HQ to the ISAF base at Kabul International Airport (KAIA). I had met Bess the previous month whilst taking an escorted ride from KAIA back to HQ. We got stuck in traffic along with Imran for two hours due to some roads being blocked. I felt a bit antsy as we went through a number of back streets trying to find a short cut. At times we were stuck in severe traffic. On one occasion, we went against the flow of traffic on a one-way street. The local drivers were not impressed. All I could think was that stuck in traffic, we were sitting ducks for anyone who wanted to attack us. Eventually the two soldiers manning the vehicle just gave up and took the long way home. When I saw the walls of HQ, I had never been so grateful to see concrete.

Imran seemed to be having some sort of attitude with me. I don't know if it was personal or just the stress of the job. We had never had any issues before and I had appreciated the manner in which he left the office well organized when I took over at Lashkargah.

Errol explained that they needed someone to make a Dari-English translation. The translators were not available due to other duties, therefore, he wanted me to call Imran and ask him to do it.

I called and informed Imran that Errol needed a translation. What I got was a dose of attitude.

"Why don't you do it? Why are you calling me?"

"Well I don't' speak Dari and you do."

"You have lived in this country for two years and you can't speak the language? Why haven't you learnt it?

"Well first of all, *none* of the FTMLs speak the language, not just me. You are from Pakistan and you do. Secondly, I am not asking you to do this, Errol is."

"But why are you asking me? Why don't you do it?"

"You know I don't speak Dari and Errol is asking you to do it." At this point, I was trying to maintain my civility."

Errol overhearing the conversation, motioned with his hand, "Give me the phone."

"Hey Imran. Our translators are transitioning from HQ to KAIA. We need this translation in a hurry. Can you help us out?"

It took Imran about a second to say yes. There was no lip or questions about Errol's Dari ability. I couldn't understand if I had told him that the request was coming from Errol, why the fucking attitude? However, he shut to fuck up and obliged once Errol spoke to him directly.

A few days later, when he entered the office just prior to the conference, I just looked at him and then looked away, refusing to acknowledge him. I didn't know what his problem was but I was not in the mood for his unwarranted attitude.

Some time later, I theorized that perhaps he had had such requests before from others who were being paid to do their job not have him do it for them. I could have been wrong but his unreasonable rudeness had rubbed me the wrong way.

I moved over to Green Acres and shared my room with Jake, a very nice, friendly guy. He had worked in Canadian TV and at some point in the eighties had worked with Jim Bard. Bard was the first TV professor I ever had back in 1988 when I started my Journalism program at Humber College. Jake snored a bit and when he drank – LORD!!! It was like a train and no amount of shouting or banging on the furniture could wake him up.

The meeting was the usual bi-annual conference. However, to Errol's credit, we now slept and conducted the conference at a decent hotel. None of sleeping at ISAF crap which was not too comfortable. We also had access to the bar. Samanta mentioned to me that Tobago had once been a Latvian colony around the 1600s or so. I thought she was tanked up on Vodka. Although tired and drunk, I had to check it on the net and turns out she was right. Amazing how little they teach us about our own country.

All the men seem quite taken with Samanta. She is a pretty blonde, however, I think if one were to pass her in downtown Toronto or London, you wouldn't give a second glance. There is something about this enclosed Afghan environment that women just seem to be hotter. I wonder if we the men look hotter to them as well.

After the conference, my flight continued to be delayed. By this time Tayeba had gone on holiday. I simply enjoyed the extra time and bed at the hotel.

Finally I booked a private flight to depart around mid-November. The flight would depart around 7:30 am.

I got to the airport and got through most of the checks fairly quickly. Seems there is less hustle when it's not a weekend. I checked in really quickly but there was a huge line to go through one door for the departure lounge. At one point I noticed a guy talking to the fellow in front of me. As we got closer to a barrier which forced the line to narrow down. He just plain stepped in front of me. This is something Afghans love to do. They simply can't line up. However, with a lot of expats in the airport, they usually get told off. Especially as some of these guys are ex-Speical Forces or Security – they don't fuck around. I'm not security but like a lot of expats here I am not in the mood for this bold-faced line cutting.

I said to the fellow, "Hello. Excuse me. I am next in line.

"I am talking to my friend."

"I don't give a fuck who you are speaking to. The line starts back there," pointing towards the back of the long que. He wasn't as big as me, however, I know that sometimes it's the less dangerous looking guys who are really dangerous.

He stepped to the side and hung his bag on the barrier, "Why don't you shut your mouth."

"Well I am not going to shut it. So what the fuck is going to happen now!!"

We both gave each other a stare down and the other Afghans in the line simply looked. After a few seconds he took his bag, stepped behind muttering away in his language. The Afghans were just looking and smiling. I figured I was getting cursed at. All I could think was go ahead and curse at me, just don't hit me from behind.

Anyway, after the obligatory delay, a few hours later I was off to Helmand.

There was a bit of a problem with me staying back late when I got to the office. The new PSYOPS Head, Major Sarah Colt was at another Camp. She had actually arrived before my leave and we had been introduced. The others arrived after I had departed. They decided that when they left the office at night so should I. I explained I had security clearance and that this had never been a problem before. However, I wasn't a white Canadian. I was a brown guy with a Trinidadian accent and I guess my ID didn't mean fuck all. They explained that it could be sorted out when Major Colt returned. Therefore, I just had to be inconvenienced for a few days. When Major Colt got back, she explained that it was ok. I am wondering why the fuck a Canadian with the same security clearance as them needs to wait to find out if he can stay back and use his computer late at night in the office. This dumb ass attitude of not being to look past the colour of my skin despite being a NATO vetted citizen is getting on my nerves.

I get the odd response, "Well you know what the enemy looks like." They have brown soldiers in their army and sadly some of them are treated like that as well. Earlier this year, a British Corporal of Pakistani descent, told me that while on patrol, the commanding officer asked her to give up her gun. She had to explain to him that she was a British soldier and that was just not something you do when outside in a war zone.

Tayeba had scheduled a holiday shortly after my return. However, due to my flight delays, he ended up leaving before I arrived. The new PSYOPS team arrived, saw an unoccupied desk and just emptied it of my belongings. I wonder if they thought they were just lucky to have that particular internet connection with no army blockings just by pure luck. I therefore had to introduce myself and ask that anything taken from my desk to please be returned. I have learnt that lesson and now in the top draw is a sheet stating who the desk belongs to and who I am.

Matt, an American also joined the team in Helmand during my absence. A tall, lanky fellow with short brown hair from New York, he was friendly enough for the first week and then I noticed he just became cold. He would barely say hello or look at me. I eventually figured out it was because in my absence he would stay up late and have chats with his girlfriend on Skype. My usual late presence in the office apparently now inhibited that. I'm sorry for him but where the hell am I supposed to go? I was there for months before he arrived. I sympathize with his plight but I have got my own problems.

A week after I arrived, I messed up in a top security room. This is basically the room where our PSYOPS Commander sits with most of his crew. There is also a top-level form of internet communication known as ISAF Secret which basically means the Taliban can't tap into your messages. I wasn't thinking and tried to download a harmless file on my extractable hard disk. You just don't do that on ISAF Secret computers. They didn't know but I tried to get help and when they realized what I was doing, security had to very politely confiscate and delete my drive. Goodbye to all that sweet football and boxing that took years to accumulate.

A week later, they had a mini freak when they realized that I was downloading torrents. Their computers are connected to my net and again this is a security issue. I politely explained this is a stand-alone satellite for *me* and if it was such an issue, they had the option to disconnect themselves. They explained that I shouldn't download torrents anyway and that they could confiscate my cables and eventually have me leave the camp. I stood my ground for about a day but then I realized that I need the office more than they need me, in addition, there was no way my boss would support me in such an argument. Everything more or less went back to normal, however, Major Colt, although polite was never quite the same after that. Pity, because I think she is a genuinely nice woman and loved the way she used to dance and sing around the office. Nice to see somebody other than me doing it. However, now she wont even make eye contact with me unless I speak to her. Other than that she is still her pleasant self.

The person who runs our office here in Lashkargah along with Major Colt is Captain Allison Ross. She is a tall broad-shouldered woman. When she has a problem with the soldiers or the Afghan journalists, she is not adverse to shouting at them. I can't help but notice that of all the Commanders we have had, she is the only one who needs to shout.

As I allow the soldiers one computer to feed off my internet, they often browse sites blocked by the British army and the occasional porn. Someone gave their computer a virus and it had to be sorted out. A few days later, one of the young soldiers was showing the other lads some sexy photos of his girlfriend. Captain Ross went nuts on them and explained that if anymore porn was viewed, they would have that particular net access cut off. Although it was explained to her that it was not a porn site, she did not seem to actually listen or care.

The Afghan men in general seem to have a problem with a female boss but I guess because of the money they suck it up and handle it. About a week after the porn incident she blew up at the local journalists in the office.

She showed them a news item that had been translated from English to Dari. Although quite long in Dari it was about half the length in English.

"We might be English but we are not stupid. If you cannot do proper translations, we'll put you out on patrol somewhere and you can get SHOT!!!"

Not a man said a word. They took the scolding in silence.

Two other members of the team I enjoy chatting with are Garth and Kapil. Garth is a medium built black fellow. He is Jamaican British and recognised my Trini accent right away. I honestly thought when I slow down and speak properly, it would not be that easy to distinguish but I guess not for a West Indian. Garth and his wife had done about twenty-three thousand pounds the previous year selling women's lingerie and

Brazilian bikinis from the computer at the kitchen table. So they were going to make a more serious effort this year.

Kapil is a slim, handsome fellow with short, black hair. If there are no women in the office, he will look at us, smile and fart hard. One morning about a month after his team had arrived. The alarm went off at about 6:00 am. This usually meant a rocket attack. We all came out, sleepy, standing in front of our tents. I looked at Kapil, "You farted and set off an alarm, didn't you?"

In December I was getting ready for my leave – Bangkok and Bali.

I met some of the other FMTLs in Kabul as they too were getting ready to head out on their holidays. We had a new addition, Abigail from Scotland. She had been brought in to replace Allan, whose contract was not renewed. Management believed that at times he was not actually at the Kandahar base and had taken one of the many flights available to be elsewhere. Not too hard when most of your work is done on the computer. But difficult if the Chief wants to speak via skype and you background looks like a hotel room. I never got the exact details but he was gone and Abigail was in. When I was introduced to her, I got a very serious "male vibe." She was extremely mannish. When I met her again, I took a serious look, observing her big hands and Adam's Apple and came to the conclusion that this was a MAN!!!

Somehow, they had hired a transsexual. The other guys came to the same conclusion. Michael was part of the panel that gave her the job. Apparently, they looked at her CV and spoke to her over the phone. I don't have a big issue with it. Sure it was a shock but this is a changing world and so be it. Working with a transexual is one thing but in Afghanistan with a lot of traditional men – good luck. Some of them might even like it.

She will work in Kandahar. Apparently, she's very experienced and seems like quite a nice person.

Chapter 19

What the Hell Is Wrong with Looking Like a Pakistani?

January-March 2011

Post Bali, I stayed at another hotel until I returned to Lashkargah. It was reasonably modern and cheaper than some of the options I had been using before. I am always welcome to stay at HQ. But after suffering in a tent for months at a time, I look forward to the bedroom, privacy and cable TV when I am in Kabul.

I would walk out on the main road sometimes to buy some goods from a store or walk in a nearby park. As one exits the neighbourhood of the hotel, there is a huge roundabout. On two occasions I was stopped by a police officer who asked to see my ID. I showed them my ISAF ID which is usually good enough. But they insisted on seeing my passport which I happened to have been walking with. When I asked why the ISAF identification was not good enough, the Dari response is "You look like a Pakistani."

This has been the answer both times and on each occasion, I respond, "And what the hell is wrong with looking like a Pakistani!?"

One lesson that I learnt after about four odd months in Afghanistan was to be clean shaven in Kabul. At the camp, I usually walk around looking like whatever the hell I feel like. However, there are plain clothes officers on the street and they often stop the private taxis I am in because I guess I have that insurgent look when I am unshaven. I give my ISAF ID and the driver explains who I work for. It became so regular by mid-2010 that if I was on the phone, I would not even stop speaking, I would give the ID to the driver, who would do the talking while I focussed on my telephone conversation.

The sound of bombs while I sleep has become the norm whilst in Lashkargah. When I was in Kunduz, we were well outside the city so I never heard them. However, as we are actually located in Lashkargah, I have heard a number of bombs during the last few months. I wake up and slowly count to sixty, checking to see if the alarm will go on. It never does and I go back to sleep.

However, in February, I heard a massive boom!!! I woke up with my heart thumping in my chest. I counted to sixty, then a hundred, three hundred and finally six hundred. I simply could not calm down. So I just breathed and tried to relax. It took about ten minutes to calm down properly and then back to sleep.

When I went to the office later, I asked Tayeba what the hell had happened. He explained that the explosion was about a kilometre away. The local Afghan Bomb Disposal Unit was at hand, there were two bombs. They had diffused the first bomb but had been unsuccessful with the second.

The Hand Over took place in late March. As the old team left in came the new. I missed the actual exchange as I was on leave again, this time to Egypt. I don't have much to do with the new Commander. However, his deputy, Captain Smithers and I see a lot more of each other. It's Smithers who does most of the ordering around the office.

I think we got off on the wrong foot when some ISAF TV crewmen were sent to do some stories in Lashkargah. I was supposed to organise their accommodations and names with security prior to their arrival. However, upon returning from leave, there was our FMTL conference in a week's time. It made no sense to fly out and then back especially with the usual delays. I therefore, stayed back and by the time the conference was over along with a few days of flight delays, I had been away for almost a month. About two days before my actual return, I sent the PSYOPS staff at Helmand an email to please accommodate the TV crew. Smithers responded saying they had actually, already arrived just prior to the email and they were trying to understand who they were and sort things out. Seeing that the PYSOPS team gets so much material from my department, I cannot understand why there isn't easier communication. It was obvious from the tone of his email and when I met him in person that they would have appreciated a heads up. He is quite right but no one had confirmed with me exactly when they were coming. This is not really Smithers' problem and I guess I look like a bit of a dick. However, this is what communication is like in Afghanistan despite our massive staff and all this sexy technology.

As the weeks rolled by Captain Smithers seemed rather observant of the time that I spent on the net and that I watched movies at night. I think he just didn't want to leave the brown guy alone in the office. But I am Canadian with the correct clearance. "I have never seen someone spend so much time as you do on the net or watching movies."

I would think to myself, it's 10:00 pm, what the fuck else is there to do and how is it your fucking business?

There is a very funny fellow from Manchester, Kevin. He had us cracking up in the office when it was just the guys, telling us about how he and his mate had met women off the internet forum chats in the nineties. He explained that how on one occasion, they were waiting at the bus stop for a girl called Janet.

"This beautiful blonde walks off the bus. We look at her, 'Janet?' She shakes her head and walks on. Then this fat chick comes off right behind her and with a heavy voice and big smile says, 'I am Janet.' I run down the street telling my mate. I am just going to buy a pack of cigarettes."

His mate looked at him in a panic, "'But you'll come back, yeah?'"

"''Sure.' But I never fucking went back."

We all laughed hysterically, the joke made even funnier by that sing song Manchester accent he has.

You try to fake it but eventually the PSYOPS team realizes that you are not that busy. They then see your position sometimes advertised by ISAF and are in awe of the salary. You can sense a bit of bitterness. It's completely understandable, they work hard, sometimes very long hours, compounded by guard duty in intense heat. I don't usually come in before 10 am. I often take a nap after lunch and then late at night, I chill by watching a movie or TV show.

I should explain that I do actually work but after you send in the radio report, you only have about two stories a week to edit. If I edit a story in a few hours, I then have the rest of the day free. Sure, I look up potential stories on the internet, but you don't need hours for that. Occasionally, there is a project from HQ and I am a little busier but my days are not that stressful.

Why then is the question that begs to be asked are we given this job and paid so much? The PSYOPS team is an important part of any war tool. Most of the other civilians get two weeks off every six months, public holidays from both Afghanistan and your home country are added. Therefore, it's possible to get three weeks or even more off. This sounds fine in theory. But only people who actually live in these camps can actually understand how tedious and depressing the life can become after a while. I refer to it as a "glorified prison." It's a dry, dusty, mundane environment (except for the cold winters), mitigated by access to the net and satellite TV.

Leave is much appreciated by civilians. However, many of us feel depressed during the last 24 hours before returning to Afghanistan. I personally feel as if there is a heavy weight on my chest. It reminds me of my youth in Trinidad & Tobago when I would sit in the traffic on the way to school in the mornings. I would have the occasional feeling of dread and depression. Well in terms of Afghanistan, there was nothing occasional about it. It was terrible and I would wonder if I could get ill. I had heard others say they were sitting in the airport and seriously considered running away. And some did. My department understood the problem and gave us a tremendous amount of leave. We received two days per month in addition to two weeks and public holidays. It worked out to 72 odd days which was taken in portions, most of us travelling about four times a year.

In early 2011, I had actually broken a piece of tooth just at the end of my Thai holiday. I returned to Kabul and was told that I required cosmetic surgery and would have to travel out of country. One could not quantify my joy as I made plans to go to Istanbul, my old stomping grounds. For some reason, the dentist had problems taking the x-ray properly and had to do it three times. In all I spent an additional 10 days in Turkey, most of it having fun, going to the cinema and eating decent food. This was covered by my Sick Leave so my holiday time was actually extended.

Therefore, we may not be overworked but what CJPOTF gets in return is a well-trained staff that does not run away. If you have to hire someone new, it could take six months to advertise, interview and hire, another six months to have them vetted and then they still have to be trained.

Most soldiers are out of here in six months but our team is here for years. At least half of them have been here for more than three years.

It may sound like we have it too easy but I firmly believe the generous leave is the only reason that none of us have ever fled.

Thus as the months have passed by, there is the odd comment in addition to Captain Smithers. There is a Non-Commissioned Officer (NCO) sitting in the far corner of the office, who loves to play with his moustache and look at photos of smoking pipes on the internet. If I come in at 10, he sometimes mutters "Good afternoon" under his breath. Yet there is never a facetious comment when they receive my Atmospherics on a weekly basis which is probably better than theirs.

Chapter 20

Acute Sufferance and Fucking a Donkey

As 2012 commenced, I began to feel the excitement regarding my imminent departure from this country. Like a lot of the civilians, I am here because I was offered a job. Many of us live in austere conditions and we do it for the money.

We count the days for our leave and the end of our contract. However, there is a flip side to the coin. For the Afghans this is not a job to be tolerated. This is their life. They are doing the best they can to survive a vicious Taliban group whilst being ordered around by foreign soldiers from time to time.

I have been here for almost three years, the Brits come for just six months, yet one can see evidence of their frustration in the washrooms. When closing the toilet doors you can observe what seems to be dried splotches all over the inside of each door. The cleaning staff has become quite fed up of this and there have been threats of simply taking the doors off their hinges. I do not enjoy the prospect of using these toilets without doors.

One's notion of this country can be a bit limited if all you see are movies and the news reports on TV. You get the impression it's a disorganized, crazy, Muslim country. However, their history is much more than just ultra conservative Muslims. Once upon a time Afghanistan was a country where the people lived a very western existence. It was part of the Hippie Trail from the 1950s to the late 70s. Europeans, Americans and many others would travel from Iran, Afghanistan, Pakistan, India and Nepal. The women wore the latest fashions including mini skirts. They would put on their makeup and boogie away at the local nightclubs. There was a bloody coup by the

Communists in 1978 and the Afghans have been suffering acutely ever since.

The Russians eliminated the Afghan President in late 1979 and assisted in setting up a new regime supported by the Russian soldiers. A full-fledged war ensued for the next nine years. The end of the war did not mean that Afghanistan had a stable existence then along came the Taliban in 1994. By 1996 they were in charge of most of the country and continued to so until the US led invasion five years later.

Theirs was a brutal regime that made Iran look like Disneyland. As one reporter in Lashkargah told me, "It was normal to see people beheaded live on national TV. But we did have a low crime rate. My uncle parked his car in front of our house on the street. There was two hundred and fifty thousand dollars in the trunk and no one touched that car all night."

I remember Aysel explaining that she had had a driver that she had used years before when she needed to get around in Kabul. His right arm was limp and sort of useless. He explained that during the Taliban regime, his father was fighting against them but he lived in Kabul. He was stopped in the street by the police in 1999 and they discovered a *Titanic* DVD on him. They took him to the local jail and tortured him. He no longer had full use of his right arm.

I was a little confused, "They didn't like the movie?"

"No. He had the movie with him so they tortured him."

"Why because they don't like the movie Titanic.?" I was still confused.

"No. It was illegal to watch movies or TV. So they tortured him. But he was actually grateful. He said they could have killed him 'but they only hurt my arm.'"

This situation has been even more unbearable for the older women who remember the freer times of the sixties and seventies. Even with the intervention of ISAF and greater rights many of them are subjugated throughout the land even worse in the more far-flung areas outside of Kabul. Being stoned to death or beheaded is not uncommon in this country. A young woman can be stoned by the village for having the temerity to refuse an arranged marriage. There are stories of some women disfiguring themselves to look less attractive and therefore discourage harassment from men.

Post-Taliban, there has been certainly some improvement despite men, women and children being killed every year by the hundreds. Democracy has been promoted along with billions being spent on Afghanistan's infrastructure and of course increased avenues for women in terms of education and work.

So as some of us bemoan our existence here the Afghans understandably are perhaps more pissed. You truly never know when you step out of your house that day if it will be your last. This is compounded by foreigners who sometimes talk down to you and order you around in your own country. Some people understandably get fed up.

There are the occasional straws that break the camel's back.

Terry Jones, a pastor of a small church in Florida, burnt a copy of the Quran on March 20, 2011. Jones believed that the Muslim faith promotes violence. He and a few of his followers had a mock trial and then set the Quran on fire. Not surprisingly, this did not go down well with the Muslim community at large.

Mazar-e-Sharif is a reasonably quiet place. Some ISAF staff and soldiers laughingly call it "the resort." No one was laughing a few days later when protestors stormed a UN building and killed seven people, four Nepalese security guards and three civilians in retaliation for Jones' actions.

There were protests through out the country and Tayeba got caught up in it a few days after the slaughter in MeS. He was on his way to work when he encountered a protest. Someone identified him as the guy "who works for the foreigners." They chased him, throwing rocks at him and hitting him on the back. He managed to outrun them and escape. Looking at Tayeba's slightly portly physique, I am confused as to how he could outrun any mob.

When he came to work that day with the assistance of one of the translators, he explained what had happened. He had problems sitting and walking because of the stones he had been hit with. I really should have let him go home early but because it was a three-way conversation and I was in shock, it did not occur to me until much later.

Fast forward to March 11, 2012, almost a year later, Sergeant Robert Bales, went into the Panjwai District of Kandahar in the early hours of the morning and murdered sixteen civilians, nine of them children, some just babies. Six others were wounded.

The Afghan government wanted him tried in their country where the crime had taken place. The US government said he would be tried by a military court in their country. Not surprisingly, the US government got what they wanted.

Afghans in general were understandably outraged. This was just another example of the foreigners abusing their rights in their own country. The local radio reporters who sit in front of me do not usually have much to say about these matters. But a day later when they saw the photos of the dead, they expressed themselves. Ali, a short, thickset fellow, with a classic broomstick moustache, looked at me and then the photos in a rage, "You will see! You will see what will happen! Something will happen."

Something certainly did. I left roughly two weeks later to prepare for leave from Kabul. Just three days after exiting the camp an Afghan National Army soldier pulled into the entrance of the PRT on March 26. He opened fire, killing two soldiers and wounding one. There is a sort of a mini canon about fifty metres away from the front of the gate precisely for this kind of occurrence. The soldiers opened fire and finished off the attack. He had to have known that was basically a suicide mission. What scared me when I heard about it was that I was standing at that very gate just about three days before. Of course I dodged that one but I want to believe had I actually been there he would have gone for the soldiers first and not me. Perhaps a bit of a selfish thought but they have guns, I don't.

This was a more brazen effort by the ANA no less. However, such attacks have been known to happen over the last few years usually due to the frustration of locals believing that they are being ruled in their own land.

Despite this, the Afghan government is working hard to have a more professional ANA and Afghan National Police (ANP) with the eventual withdrawal of ISAF troops by 2014.

Professionalism amongst both the ANA and the ANP has been a challenge in itself. Many are illiterate. Poorly paid, a lot of them have no problem soliciting bribes. A great number simply do not have the sophistication nor education required for the job. When we exchange notes from amongst our contacts, we hear stories that in the rural areas sometimes the ANP will pass by and start to have sex with a family's donkey. When the family comes outside, they tell them "We can do this because we are with the ANP."

However, if the government does not give these men a job then the Taliban will.

Chapter 21

Challenges and Another Close Call

March-April 2012

This is a job where you should expect challenges. What Command expects is that you can use your initiative and handle them whilst they support you as they can.

I soon realized that 2012 would be no different than previous years. First of all, we had been trying to find a replacement for Hadad. It would not be a quick process, we would first have to place an ad, interview the candidates and then have them vetted. Therefore, from beginning to end you were looking at around two months maybe more.

After some dismal applicants, a young woman by the name of Roqia came in early March. She seemed the best of the lot. She wasn't amazing but I figured as I usually rewrote everything, once she wrote comprehensibly it would be ok. She was quite wrapped up in typical Afghan fashion during the interview, only her face was visible. Once she had been accepted, we asked her to be patient regarding the vetting.

A few weeks later, I was on my way to Kabul to go on leave. I occasionally get some static at the Lashkargah airport for no other reason than I am brown. And this is from people who are brown.

On this occasion, after the obligatory search of the baggage. I was stopped by an employee literally at the entrance of the small building known as the airport. He could see no visa in my passport. I explained that I worked for ISAF. We had no visas but the ISAF ID was enough.

He looked at me. "Can I do this in your country?" He then pointed to a nearby building for me to go and speak to the people there for permission to go on the plane. Just as I was entering, I saw a woman exiting, her face covered, she exclaimed, "Veersen."

Who the hell is this? I wondered.

I looked at her, my eyebrows furrowed together expressing my bewilderment.

"It's me Roqia."

We exchanged greetings and I explained why I had come to this office. She spoke to the men in Dari and they nodded.

"It's ok," she said. "You can come with me."

I looked at her, a bit surprised.

"I explained to them that you are my boss, you are Canadian and you work for ISAF."

I was happy for the assistance. But I remained confused as to how these officials could be so clueless about an ISAF ID and as to why the employees with my kind of clearance did not have a visa. It's not like I was kitchen staff.

We had a nice chat before the flight. She told me that she would stay with her family in Kabul before going to Uzbekistan where she had accepted a job with a Non-Government Organization. I was a little surprised by this.

"But what about the job we offered you?"

"No of course that is the most important. I will come back immediately?"

"Are you sure you can do this?"

She assured me that it would be no problem. I did however, have my doubts.

As we got our bags upon our arrival in Kabul, I realized she was less hidden from the world. She was wearing jeans and a sweater covered by a thin long robe with a slit on either side. Her face was visible and she was wearing a fair degree of makeup.

"Where are you staying?"

"I have a hotel reservation."

Oh that is not necessary. My brother is picking me up and you are very welcome to stay at our house."

"Oh thank you so much but ISAF is paying so it's no big deal."

She insisted and then I insisted and she eventually accepted my response. I was actually telling a bit of a lie. I could stay at HQ with accommodations provided but ISAF was not paying for my hotel. As I yearned for a comfortable room, I always took a hotel in Kabul. This was more dangerous but after months in a tent, I didn't give a fuck. I needed a good bed and a comfy hotel room.

Upon my return in April, we had the conference just a few days later. There was no point in going to Helmand and I was more than happy for the extra time in Kabul.

As usual we had fun in our spare time chatting at lunch or drinking away at night. The new Commander for CJPOTF is a huge seven foot American, Colonel Willard. He seems to be an easy-going guy. He doesn't need to do 8 am briefings every day. The new Media Chief is also an American, Lieutenant Col. Reeves. He has made it clear Journalism is not his background. However, he will listen to us and support us as we need it. This new Command seems a lot more relaxed than the previous one with whom we got the impression that they were just Karl's buddies looking to humble us and put us in our place.

We had been told that if we went on leave to arrive 24 hours before the conference. I was going to Egypt and I thought no frigging way am I losing a day and made sure to return a day later just a few hours before the start. I figured I could get some sleep on the plane.

Just before I left, Errol realized what I had done. I feigned ignorance "But I will be in the office before the conference starts."

Errol was a bit pissed and understandably so. "You know what you did. You deliberately disobeyed me. But you have done it and there is nothing I can do about it now."

I continued to play dumb but he was quite right. However, I figured I am the jackass somehow always getting the short end of the stick when it comes to accommodations at a PRT, I sure as hell am not losing a day of leave.

Upon my return from leave, I dropped my bags off at the hotel and rushed to the conference. I was exhausted.

When it was my turn to speak. I told the Commander that I would stand as I had been sitting for the last 24 hours. The truth was I didn't trust myself to keep sitting as I might fall asleep.

About half an hour later as someone else was speaking, I drifted off and my snoring woke me up. My jerked up immediately and I saw Errol glaring at me, I glared back as if unaware of what had just happened. This was exactly why he had wanted me in 24 hours prior to the conference.

There was a Romanian woman from the Civilian Personnel Office sitting next to me. She was slim, pretty with medium length, dark, black hair in her mid to late thirties. She obviously was not aware of the dress protocol in Afghanistan or didn't care. She had a few buttons of her blouse undone and was exhibiting ample cleavage. A heavenly sight for men in Afghanistan whether you're local or foreign. As she chatted, I looked at her pretending I was interested and that it was her face that I was really looking at. After the meeting, all the guys mentioned how much they appreciated the view. Seeing that we live in Afghanistan, God bless her.

The next few days after the conference, we all used the time to take care of personal matters and any paperwork that had to be tended to. I noticed that Imran would not make eye contact with me or greet me. I remembered he had been a bit rude a few months back when being requested to do a translation. I had no idea what the fuck his problem was. But I really didn't care.

I had been using the same taxi service since my arrival in Kabul in 2009. However, on the day that I went on leave they really fucked up. I usually had a pickup reservation for 5 am or would call them at 4:30 am. If it was the latter, the phone might ring for a while as the man in charge was sleeping.

On this day I had a 5 am reservation. I called at 4:30 am to confirm with them but no one answered the phone. I waited and at 5:10 started calling again. No matter how much I called and how many times the phone rang there was no answer. At 5:25 I began to panic. Getting into the Kabul airport is stressful being late and trying to fight with that crowd was a frightening thought.

I was now stressed because there would be some degree of traffic and getting to the airport after six meant it would be around 7:30 or so before I got to check in for an 8 am flight.

The guard called an alternative service for me and said it would take fifteen minutes to arrive. Five minutes later, the dicks that I had been calling for almost an hour called back. The lame ass excuse was that the car came and did not see me. Which I knew was rubbish.

"I have bee here since 4:25 am. How the hell couldn't he see me on an empty street in front of the hotel. There was no fucking car. And you have been sleeping and wouldn't answer the phone.

"I am going to miss my flight!!!"

"I am sorry sir. What can I do for you?"

"Do you own a plane!!??

"I am going to miss flight. Do you own a plane!!??"

He continued to apologize and I hung up the phone.

I will never know how it worked out but the taxi arrived and got me to the airport at 6. I entered the first check at 6:25. There were only two people ahead of me and the one X-ray machine was working. I was through in 10 minutes. Amazingly the next three checks had no line and I was at the check-in desk at 6:50 and in the Departure Lounge at 7:10. Whenever I was on time, I never breezed through the checks like this. I realized that if you could find a window just after the initial early morning rush, this is what it was like. However, I had no intentions of doing anything last minute in a Kabul airport.

I therefore, was now using a new service. I had built a rapport with some of the drivers from the previous company but I was determined that they should never get my business again.

On Sunday April 15, I left KAIA after lunch and made my way back to the hotel. Just after 1 pm, I heard what sounded like gunshots. I looked around and just saw people running in every direction. The driver punched it and we were off. I ducked down and was confused as to why kilometre after kilometre, I could still hear the gunfire. I wouldn't be Trini if I wasn't a just a bit nosy so I would raise my head from time to time to see what was going on. At this point all the cars were speeding to their destination. My driver was zooming in between cars. I felt like I was in the middle of a chase scene in a movie.

As we arrived at my hotel, I jumped out and wished him luck getting back to the office. The guards recognized me as a guest and this time there was no security check. I was rushed to the basement along with the other guests.

The Head of Hotel Security explained that this was a coordinated attack throughout the city. He explained that we had ample security and that we should be safe in the basement. The phone signals were dead and with my computer up in my room, I could not access the internet and I did not have a smart phone. They brought snacks and drinks for us and a lot of the guests just chatted and got to know each other. I got friendly with Alex, a Canadian living in Montreal. He was nice enough to lend me his computer and I sent a message to the office. I could only imagine how they must have been worrying with no word from me.

At around 7:30 pm we were allowed to return to our rooms and access the restaurant for dinner. Alex and I continued to bond. His background was finance and he worked for a local NGO. He had studied in Russia and spoke the language fluently. I was glad to have a buddy at the hotel as it mitigated the boredom.

The next day the office made contact with me. Apparently, no one bothered to check their email. As I was the only one who chose to stay in a hotel off base, I was the only one they had to worry about.

Chapter 22

Flashlight Prick and Kicking my Bed

April-May 2012

Back at camp roughly a week after the Kabul attack, I once again had to be inconvenienced due to the colour of my skin.

Although my ID meant I could go forgo the usual search, they would usually do it anyway. On this occasion I was being searched by a young fellow probably less than half my age. They then looked at me a little apologetically and told me that although my ID was fine, they were being observed by their superiors behind the canon fifty metres away and they had been told that I should be "escorted" into the camp.

About five minutes later Matt appeared, he looked around and then exclaimed in astonishment, "That's Veersen!

"Veersen, didn't you tell them that you are Canadian!"

"I did but no one seems to take me seriously."

"Veersen you know why. It's because you're not white."

"The thought had crossed my mind."

I could not help but notice upon my return some sort of wet sploshes that had dried up on the toilet doors. I mentioned it to some of the soldiers and they laughed. As they put it many a soldier just felt like jerking off in the toilets and depositing the net result on the door. The cleaning staff had gotten quite frustrated and again threatened to pull all doors off the toilets. I could not bear the thought of using the toilet without a door and thank God it never happened.

Despite the recent attack in Kabul, I tried to keep calm. I would go on leave in late June, return in July and in mid-September that was it. Goodbye.

Sometimes I sit outside the office and look around at the gravel and the small electric turbines. I cannot envisage a life where I will never see these again. However, I know the time is nigh. I simply feel like a prisoner on the verge of release.

Upon my return, I walked into my tent only to find out that during my absence the whole damn tent had been converted to women only. The ladies were quite calm and unperturbed by presence and explained that my belongings had been moved along with the other occupants to "another tent."

I ran over to some sort of office that shared its space with the Post Office and a huge, friendly sort of South Pacific Native black fellow gave me directions to my new abode. It was actually next door to the ladies. Thank God, I had left nothing of value behind. These tents are actually quite big with about eight or more separate sleeping areas, each holding about eight people. Mine was at the very end just like the previous one for which I thanked God as it meant less traffic passing in front of our entrance and disturbing us.

I now had to put up with a fair bit of discontent regarding my snoring. I guess unbeknownst to me I snore. I figured it out the previous November when an officer from the sleeping area next to mine woke me up with a flashlight in my face screaming that I had kept him and his mates up all night. He suggested that I should go report myself to the local security. I was in absolute shock. I reported the matter to Major Ford. She made it clear that was not proper protocol.

"Did you get the person's name Veersen?"

"No Ma'am."

"Well then, the next time this happens, ask them for their name. Write it down. Come to us and we can have them reported. Because they certainly have no right to do this."

"Yes Ma'am."

It turned out the prick and his flashlight had exited the camp with his team so there was no way to report him.

However, the snoring debacle was not yet over. I really wasn't aware of how bad it was. I could not believe that such a horrible sound was coming out of my face and I couldn't hear it. Very occasionally, I would snore loudly enough to wake myself up. The members of my tent understandably became a bit frustrated, one Captain in particular.

About a week after flashlight prick, he would get up and kick my bed. Thank God not me. I would of course wake up. I could have complained but I did feel somewhat responsible. I had experienced the occasional snorer in previous months and it is a pain in the ass.

My bed would get a good kicking every night. However, I noticed the same Captain didn't seem to mind playing his music at the crack of dawn when he woke up.

I did my best to adjust my sleeping position and I guess it worked because the bed was kicked less.

Roqia was accepted for her post in late May. I emailed her quite a few times and she did not respond. I must say I was not surprised. I was always curious as to how she would leave a job in Uzbekistan and immediately start with us. After about two weeks, she emailed Tayeba and told him to tell me that she would be in Afghanistan one week later. I could only shake my head. I sent her another email asking how was it she could communicate with Tayeba but not me. Again, no answer.

Only desperation for a replacement had made me tolerate her for that long. I immediately decided that we would blacklist her. She would therefore, never be eligible for an ISAF job again. Silly girl, all she had to do was say she had accepted another job and we could have moved on.

Ever since Hadad's departure Tayeba had had to step up and do the Print Reporter's job. He would usually get a translator to verbalize the English version and I would type. They were quite impressed with my typing speed but I am a journalist after all.

His English has improved to the point where we can have conversations about work or other matters. Sometimes he impishly jokes that I should stay in Afghanistan and marry Roqia.

Imagine my shock when in early June he mentioned that I am on Afghan TV every night. The previous year I had met an Afghan reporter, Abdul, who works for the TV branch of CJPOTF. We had chatted and it was he who had come down in April from Kabul to do some stories. He has always been very pleasant to me and even took me out for lunch the last time I was in Kabul. One day as I exited a flight in Lashkargah he and other passengers were waiting to board. We quickly greeted each other and exchanged a few pleasantries. What I did not know was that he had filmed the passengers disembarking, myself included. Now this short clip was in the opening credits of a Kabul TV station's newscast every night. I suppose it's not a big deal. However, this is a war zone and the idea is to be subtle and covert if possible.

Chapter 23

A Death in the Family and an Unpopular Captain

June 2012

June was at hand and I was excited. I would travel to Italy and as this was on my bucket list, I was as giddy as a schoolgirl.

I arrived in Kabul well ahead of my departure date. Errol was not overly concerned about me being at the office unless he needed me. I think he just didn't want the extra traffic in his limited space. Of course I would occasionally come in for the morning debriefing and exchange notes with him.

Around 2:20 am early on Wednesday morning on June 20 my phone rang. I looked at it and realized it was a number from England. The only person who would be calling me from there would be my sister. She hardly ever called and certainly not at such an hour. My only thought was that my mother must have died and she is calling me. Oh Lord, I thought as I picked up the phone.

"Hello Viri. It's Annu. No it's not about Mummy, it's Utra."

Utra was my other sister from one of my father's post-marriage relations. I thought maybe she had been in a car accident or something worthy of a call.

She then explained that Utra had actually died the previous day. I was in shock. I made Annu repeat herself. Apparently, she had had collapsed at home and although rushed to the hospital was dead on arrival despite the best efforts of the medics and Doctors.

The connection was a bad one and we were disconnected. I called back and she explained that as Utra's family was Muslim the funeral should have been the next day. However, her husband would put it off by one day so there could be an autopsy. I knew there was no way I could get there from Afghanistan in time. Annu's passport was expiring in less than six months. She got some sort of permission to fly in and was literally running to the grave as they lowered Utra into the ground.

I enjoyed my holiday as best I could under the conditions.

With about seven weeks to go I settled into the office trying to contain myself. I knew I would have to go to Kabul a week early which to me was like pre-leave.

We had had two new additions to the office back in April, Captain Grell and a very pretty Captain Gower.

Gower was indeed a beauty, approximately 170 centimetres, slim with not an inch of body fat, long, dark brown hair and brown eyes, she naturally caught the eye of the males in the office. For the first two weeks most of the fellows would automatically have a change in body language every time she entered our office area. Some would become silent and many would have a sort of spaced out semi smile on their face.

However, I noticed that after into about a month, things seemed to have changed. No one seemed to pay as much attention to her anymore and on a few occasions, she would make a request of a soldier and when she left and closed the door they would give the finger. Whatever the problem was I figured it was not any of my business.

On two occasions, I bumped into her my mistake. I apologised but she just kept looking in the other direction. I repeated myself but she showed not indication that I was even there. It was like I was a ghost. I then realized she and I had never actually had a conversation. I wondered if she was just weird or did she perhaps have a problem with me?

On one occasion I made a mistake and said she was in the Airforce. One of the soldiers went nuts. "What!!! You think that piece of filth and I are in the same category. *She* is in the Navy and *I* am in the Airforce!!!"

I immediately smiled and apologised for my faux paus.

Things got even stranger back in late April when Errol sent me an email saying he had met her at KAIA. She said she didn't know who I was. Considering she had worked in the same space as me for three weeks, used my Atmospherics and the radio reports from Tayeba, had poured her coffee about six feet from face, not to mention used my satellite internet feed, this was bizarre.

Captain Grell was pouring his coffee as I read the email. I could only laugh in disbelief. I pointed it out to him and we both laughed. I tried to explain to Errol how impossible it was for her *not* to know who I was. However, I could tell from the tone of his email that he didn't really believe me and that I should make an effort to reach out to her.

When he visited in early May seeing the operation, he then realized my point.

Her craziness aside, she can be a sight for sore eyes. On one occasion, sitting in front of me and using the net, she unzipped her pants and raised her shirt to rub her stomach. The woman simply had a beautiful, flat stomach and frontal area.

Chapter 24

Watching the Olympics Surrounded by the Taliban

July-August 2012

The London Olympics was in late June and it was a welcome distraction from my environment.

I had links on my computer but there was one tent where you could go and watch movies or play DVDs. There would always be a few men watching and even more for the premier events like the sprints.

The Trinidad & Tobago women's team had made it to the 4x100 metre relay finals. Due to their time and National Record in the semis (42.31), they seemed to have a good chance of medalling. However, they dropped the baton in the final and did not finish.

I went nuts. There was a black fellow sitting at the back of the tent and I could tell that like me he was from the West Indies.

I looked at him. "Every four years this happens. How do you a drop a baton every fucking four years."

Some of the British soldiers looked at me with a broad smile. They seemed to be amused to hear a West Indian accent come out of an Indian mouth.

"I ran the relay when I was younger and I never dropped the baton ONCE!!! How do you fuck this up every four years!?"

He and I started chatting and began naturally bonding as fellow West Indians. His name is John. It seems that he was a cricketer and footballer of note in Guyana but his father had him focus on books.

He is married with a kid in England and after giving the British Army a certain amount of years of service should get his citizenship.

It was a great Olympics for Trinidad, our best ever, a Gold, Silver and two Bronze medals.

On the night of the 100 metres, the tent was full, approximately fifteen men. I had a prime seat in the front. We were all making our predictions. Of course Usain Bolt was the favourite but there were some who though his fellow Jamaican, Asafa Powell might have a shot.

I explained to anyone who was listening that Asafa had problems with rounds and his legs seemed to get tired. Therefore, "He won't even place third."

As the athletes got ready, you could feel the tension in the room as is the norm in an explosive event like this. I looked at a Captain sitting next to me, "Technology is a helluva thing isn't it? Here we are in the middle of the desert surrounded by the Taliban and we're about to watch the 100 metres Olympic Final live from London."

"Well with our luck, they'll bomb us right now," he responded.

"Well they'll just have to wait 10 seconds."

Usain Bolt won handily. Powell got injured and finished way down the field in last place.

John and I have continued to chat and get to know each other. It is really nice to have someone with a similar cultural background as mine and I do enjoy our chats.

Chapter 25

Beheadings, a Gold Brick and My Departure

August 2012

As August came to a close, I got my handover notes ready for my replacement.

I made sure there was a document in the top draw making it clear as to whom this desk was used by. A lot of the PSYOPS team were coming to the end of their tour and some of them were gradually being replaced. One of the incoming soldiers was a sergeant I had actually met in my first week in Lashkargah. He had helped me to obtain a pillow for my bunk.

This wouldn't be Helmand province if people weren't getting slaughtered. Ali was an Asian looking fellow amongst the Afghan journalists in our office. Everyone agreed that he had a kind of Bruce Lee look about him. He would wear the traditional Afghan pants and robe very much like Bruce did in some of his movies. One day in mid-August as he sat next to my desk, he mentioned that his neighbour had been captured by the Taliban. The fellow was working for ISAF and had been travelling home to be with his family for Ramazan.

They had stopped the bus on the highway and went directly to him. They looked at the photos on his phone. "Oh so you work with the enemy. Come with us." He had obviously been sold out by someone who knew his schedule.

I thought to myself if he is lucky, he'll get a bullet to the head. I had seen videos of their decapitations and a bullet was a much better and more humane way to go.

I could see the concern on Ali's face. "I hope he will be alright."

Two days later during the height of the Ramazan celebrations, his family was called and told where to go pick him up.

When they arrived, what they found was a body that had been beaten until it turned black and three bullet holes in his chest.

Tayeba was always highly respected amongst the journalism community in Lashkargah. I was told that at certain conferences at the Governor's briefings, he would be given the VIP treatment and taken into another room. It was not uncommon for people to phone him to ask him about the Governor's plans for the future. He would get a bit pissed and tell them to ask the Governor's office.

"Why are they calling me?" he would ask me.

"Because they know you are good at your job and they respect you."

On August 27, a few hours before it was reported on CNN, Tayeba explained that the night before 17 people had been beheaded in a rural area a few kilometres outside of Lashkargah. They had been dancing and singing at a wedding. Two women and fifteen men consequently lost their heads.

Even as a foreigner I knew better than this. If you go more than a kilometre outside of Lashkargah, you're pretty much on your own. Just about anywhere at night is pretty dangerous and outside of the city is not where you want to be.

Why would anyone do something like this in a rural area in a province like this defies logic.

There are some Afghans who have capitalized well due to NATO's presence in their country. Many have been paid well and the money has flown through the economy. However, there are those who run their own business, e.g., construction and it is no exaggeration to say they make millions. Two weeks before I left the camp, I saw the local reporters in front of me laughing and talking excitedly. When I asked what had happened, they pointed to a slim, short fellow.

He had translated for a construction owner regarding getting a contract in the camp. The businessman had told the translator that if he did get the job, he would be rewarded. When notified that the contract was his, he explained that he would be back in two weeks and give the translator his reward. The gentleman kept his word, the reporter received a gold brick. I could only shake my head. I thought these things only happened in the movies.

Although my contract would end on September 18, I could actually leave on 11 days earlier because of accrued leave.

I departed Lashkargah on August 30 and the day before gave my driver Zabi some of my bags so I would not have to walk with a lot of crap when exiting for good.

I got up early that morning almost disbelieving that it was my final time to do so in this glorified football field where I had lived for 18 months.

Tayeba had told me that he would meet me in front of my tent and walk me to the gate. As I stood there with my bags, I saw Kevin walking towards the tent. I looked at him as if to greet and say farewell simultaneously. He looked at me blanky for a few seconds and then walked into the tent, never really acknowledging me. I was a bit shocked at his rudeness. We had always chatted nicely in the office. When he had left his area due to a falling out with a much larger soldier and moved into mine in the back of the tent about a month earlier, I had actually helped him bring his stuff in. I guess my relaxed schedule really did rub some people the wrong way.

Tayeba came and helped me with my bags. We walked to the gate and met Zabi outside. He gave me a big hug and wished me the best. I had really grown to respect him. He was obviously practically iconic amongst the journalism community in Lashkargah. He was a committed and hardworking journalist.

Chapter 26

Putting Up with Ignorance and a Final Goodbye

Upon my arrival in Kabul, I filled out a few forms, did some basic work and then for the last three days one of the other FMTLs took over my duties.

I did make sure that all paperwork was done as not only did I have to get paid but there was a very beautiful bonus coming my way for having spent three years with my department.

With less than a week left to leave I would still have to put up with some ignorance from the very people I was supposed to be working with.

When I had first arrived there was an American woman running the CPO that no one seemed to like. One Turkish fellow went on leave and simply did not return rather than to keep working with her. One problem he had with her was that she did not want him speaking Turkish to Turks who came in. She only wanted to hear English in the office. She seemed to have forgotten that most of the operation was being run by NATO and that French was the official language of NATO and the UN. Some wondered if she would ban French from the office as well.

A year later she was gone and replaced by a retired Romanian Colonel. He was a nice, pleasant, approachable fellow and it was he who had told me that it was illegal for them to send me from Kunduz to Helmand.

At some point the CPO office at HQ had been moved. Needing to go there, I got directions from Errol and then from others within the camp. I entered the building unable to locate it. I walked from one end to another looking for a sign that would indicate the office. I could see none.

I asked some Americans at the end of the building if they knew where it was. They did not even know *what* it was.

As I walked back the way I came. I saw a blonde woman from the CPO exit an office right next to the entrance. She was from Eastern Europe, a little heavy with glasses and medium length hair. We instantly recognized each other.

"Do you know where the CPO office is?"

"Of course. It's right here." pointing to where she had just exited, her tone indicative of a schoolteacher speaking to a thick child.

"I didn't know. There's no sign."

Again in a tone like some master speaking to a lowly servant, she looked at me, "Everybody knows where it is."

"Well not everybody because the people at the end of the building said they don't."

"Well here it is. Go!"

I gave her a firm look as if to say what the fuck is wrong with you?

She also gave me a firm look as if to indicate that I was some child that she was putting in his place.

I walked into the office and saw Jess.

"Jess! Who is that rude, fat bitch that just left the office?"

"What's wrong?"

I explained what had happened.

"Don't worry about it man."

"Well I have to worry about it. There is no sign on the door. The people in the building don't know what CPO is and she is talking to me like I'm doing something wrong. What the fuck is wrong with her?"

Jess in his usual polite way tried to calm me down.

The following day I went to KAIA for the morning briefing and just to kill some time as I really had no work to do. When entering there would be a bunch of Afghans in a wooden building that had to line up and push against each other to get through the security check. They then had to go through a separate building with an X-ray machine. Then finally they were free to enter and wait for the bus that would take them to whatever part of the compound they had to go to.

Fortunately with my ID I didn't need to line up. The guards recognizing it would call me forward. The locals were not that willing to just let me walk past them so I had to ask politely while less politely I pushed my way through the throng as they ignored me.

I did so that morning bypassed the X-ray building and pinned my ID to my chest as was the norm. As I walked to the bus stop a large Belgian soldier approached me.

"What are you doing here? That ID is for HQ, not here."

"Actually I use it for both facilities."

"Well you can't. I will let you in today but tomorrow if I see you, I won't let you enter," he said in a very authoritative tone.

"But this ID is allowed for both areas. My commander says so and I have been doing it for years."

"Well not today," he said towering over me. "And if I see you tomorrow, you won't be allowed to enter."

Rather than argue with someone who had already made up his mind, I moved on. I mentioned it to Errol who just repeated to me what I already knew. Once I explained that the soldier had not been in the listening mood, he agreed that something would have to be done.

He mentioned it at the morning debriefing. The Commander looked at one of the Belgian Colonels. "Well you are Belgian, you deal with this." He smiled and nodded. The next day there was no Belgian dick shouting down at me.

As is the norm there was a farewell ceremony for me after one of the debriefings later that week. The Commander gave me a photo of myself in Afghanistan thanking me for my service. I received a medal which was standard for anyone giving more than a year' service and also a NATO coin.

I thanked them and mentioned to the room that as I had worked in Helmand which was the opium capital of the world and that "to round myself off properly," I would be going to the cocaine capital of the world, Medellin to which I received a fair degree of laughter.

I reminisced that there would be no more sleeping in tents in sub zero weather or getting up to the sensation of snow falling on my face through the roof of the tent or having to sleep in your office to avoid sub-zero tents. The room laughed and gave me a loud round of applause. After the fact, a terrible existence can make for great story telling.

When I visited HQ the next day the bank manager saw me on the street. He realized that I was leaving and gave me a firm hug goodbye. We had developed a rapport over the years and I appreciated the gesture.

During my last 24 hours I looked around at both camps and it was a surreal feeling. I had fantasized about this moment for years. And now that it was finally here it was almost too much to believe.

On my final night I went through my usual stress about having to endure the Afghan airport. To mitigate the matter, I had sent a bag ahead by FedEx to Canada. Therefore, with two bags and a carry on, my battle to enter the airport would be less arduous.

That afternoon one of the security heads at the hotel, a local Afghan realizing that I was leaving also gave me a firm hug. We had only met a handful of times but again I appreciated the gesture.

I got my taxi at five the next morning. I went through the X-ray at the first building in a line that wasn't really that bad. The guard in front of everyone asked me for a bribe with a bright smile on his face. He kept rubbing his thumb against two fingers indicating money. I looked at the people behind me in the line and thought shouldn't you be doing this in private? I fished into my pocket and pulled out two Afghanis. I gave it to him. He looked at me in disgust and threw it at me. I guess it wasn't enough.

I crowded with the other passengers onto the bus with my three bags. I was one of the last ones to get on so I was positioned near the exit doors at the middle of the bus. I stood close to the steps trying to hold my bags steady with one hand and hold a metal bar with another so I wouldn't fall. Now we just had to line up at the front doors. Once in, most of the stress would be over.

I may have been one of the last to board the bus but now that we had to disembark, I was one of the first to exit. Of course the people at the front door had a head start but they could only hold their bags and disembark so fast. With my footlocker bag slung over my shoulders. I put my knapsack through the door first and just pulled the suitcase after me. I sprinted towards the front doors with the other passengers running behind me. This was now survival of the fittest. I had never actually been in front before and all I saw was open space. It confused me and I ran past the doors by mistake. Realizing my error, I screeched to a halt and made a U-turn for the door bags in tow. The other passengers so intent on following me also screeched to a halt Road Runner style and followed me. I was inside and simply chose the line that I wanted. On to Check In which was a smooth as silk and after thirty odd minutes of immigration and a final check at security – the Departure Lounge. I thanked the Lord God for the lack of stress made sweeter by the fact that I would never have to go through this again.

I left Kabul at approximately 8 am that morning. As the plane gained altitude, I exhaled in relief. However, I did not allow myself to get excited until I had landed in Dubai.

I had never been so happy to leave a country. I was on to a well-deserved break and an easier life but I thought of so many of the good people I had left behind in Afghanistan, a beautiful country with magnificent potential. They would have to carry on. It would take this country decades to get back to some semblance of normal.

I on the other hand now had a book to write.

CPSIA information can be obtained
at www.ICGtesting.com
Printed in the USA
LVHW030434080321
680820LV00023B/607